Called To Teach

*Breathing Spirit into
Public Education*

Lea Mathieu

Daily Bread Press
Ione, Oregon

Also by Lea Mathieu
The Literate Spirit: Suggested
Reading for Believers and Seekers

ISBN: 0-615-31106-7
ISBN-13: 978-0-615-31106-7

Published by Daily Bread Press, Ione, Oregon
www.dailybreadpress.com

Unless otherwise indicated, the Scripture quotations contained herein are from the New Revised Standard Version Bible, copyright © 1989 by the Division of Christian Education of the National Council of the Churches of Christ in the U.S.A.

Anecdotes throughout the book are from the author's own experience; however, names of students and colleagues are changed to protect their privacy.

TO

Those who teach by example, including:

Kate Frost – Shakespeare and chutzpah

Ellen Davis – Hebrew and the power of gentleness

Table of Contents

Introduction

Samuel Butler described many churchgoers well in *The Way of All Flesh*: "[T]hey would have been equally horrified at hearing the Christian religion doubted, and at seeing it practiced." This book is an invitation to my fellow teachers to bridge the common gap between faith and action by practicing instead of preaching outrageous love, generosity, wisdom, courage, and all other good things God calls us to be.

My professional calling shifted from parish ministry to teaching in public schools twelve years ago, and I initially struggled with a new kind of witness. I cannot and do not preach at school, but as a sign in my home office says, "You can preach a better sermon with your life than with your lips." This book isn't about proselytizing, which you cannot do at school for a variety of good reasons; it's about being energized by the Spirit of God to be the best Christian, teacher, and human being you can be.

Most helpful to me at the outset was Parker J. Palmer's book *The Courage to Teach*. His thoughts sparked the process that has resulted in this series of Biblical meditations in which I am only articulating what I need to know myself. I trust it will be helpful to other believers who strive to live their faith seven days a week.

Called to Teach includes 36 topics, one for every week of the typical academic year, plus special topics such as sports, death, and the challenge of secular Christmas. It may be used for group or individual discipline. If used privately, it would be helpful to keep a journal of your own experiences and thoughts concerning the topics.

Alternatively, you may meet with a group of other Christians one morning a week before the workday begins; in this case, conversation may take the place of journaling. You should each have your own book and come prepared to discuss the day's topic. What did the scripture kindle in you? Do you agree or disagree with my interpretation? What situations did it bring to mind from your own experience? These meetings would end with prayer for your own work and specific students; suggested prayers are offered with each meditation. Also included is a "daily reminder" to repeat at the beginning of each day and as needed. Liberal, conservative, evangelical, fundamentalist, Catholic, Protestant – we all share the need to live according to God's will. Invite everybody.

People who misunderstand "separation of church and state" may tell you that you can't discuss the Bible and faith within the walls of a school. Have this opinion from the U.S. Department of Education ready to hand to them:

"Teachers may … take part in religious activities where the overall context makes clear that they are not participating in their official capacities. Before school or during lunch, for example, teachers may meet with other teachers for prayer or Bible study to the same extent that they may engage in other conversation or nonreligious activities." ("Guidance on Constitutionally Protected Prayer in Public Elementary and Secondary Schools," February 7, 2003. Available on-line at www.ed.gov.)

It is *not* appropriate for you to meet in sight of students or non-participating colleagues, which could be interpreted as religious coercion. Nor is it appropriate to invite students to participate with you, as the lines of worship and teaching would potentially be blurred.

Can you wear a small cross, or have one on your desk? Can you carry a Bible with you to work? Yes, yes, and yes. But the religious symbols should be unobtrusive. For example, you cannot wear a t-shirt with "Jesus Saves" emblazoned on it. And the Bible should be read on your own time, not during class (unless you're lucky enough to teach the Bible as literature). You cannot and should not force religion on your students, but neither are you expected to leave your faith in the parking lot.

Christians can be pushy, but more often we are too timid. The Gospel is a radical invitation to new life from the root, transforming first our own spirits and then the world. Confidently fulfill your calling.

Disclaimer: I am a minister and teacher, not a lawyer, and point out that community mores differ widely; know where the lines are drawn in your district. For answers to frequently asked questions, see the excellent document by the Freedom Forum, "A Teacher's Guide to Religion in the Public Schools," recommended by the U.S. Department of Education. It is freely available on-line at www.freedomforum.org.

Teaching is hard work. Faith is hard work. We are richly blessed that God has called us to both.

Peace,

Lea Mathieu

In The Beginning: Genesis 1

"When God began to create heaven and earth — the earth being un-formed and void, with darkness over the surface of the deep and a wind from God sweeping over the water — ..." (Genesis 1:1-2)

When you look at your classroom at the beginning of the year, what do you see? In mine, the desks are in neat rows, the books are lined up on the shelves in alphabetical order, the car-pet is newly shampooed and spotless, and my lesson plan book contains not one single scribble or erasure. It's lovely, it's quiet, and it's all mine.

Then the students arrive.

This is the beginning point of creation. Until then, no matter how carefully we have prepared, a void exists in our rooms. There is no life. Invariably, the arrival of those little living creatures means changes to our expectations and plans, and certainly to our alphabetical order!

In many ways, teaching is like creating a world in our class-rooms. Where there is stillness and emptiness, life enters and creates so many possibilities. Teachers and other staff constantly adjust to the needs of dozens of unique growing, learning, struggling, suffering, beautiful children of God. The challenges never end.

The same is true of God with our world: creation is con-stant. The scripture quoted above may sound odd if you use other translations of Genesis that start out: "In the beginning when God created ..." I've used the Jewish Publication Soci-ety's 1985 translation, which recognizes that verb forms in an-cient Hebrew are not as precise as they are in most modern languages. I like this interpretation because it implies that heaven and earth are still being created. This is in keeping with other scripture that speaks of God creating each of us as we are born (see Psalms 139:13), and of recent astronomical discoveries of the present births of stars and even galaxies.

Continuous creation also recognizes that we have a role in what we become. God does not form us as robots or puppets, but as individuals with free will who are capable of charting our own course, and of influencing the development of other individuals, institutions, and ecosystems.

That implies a deep responsibility for teachers. In creating worlds of our classrooms, we are working with God in shaping life. Where there might have been a chaotic void in a student's life or mind, we have the opportunity to create order, discipline, acceptance, and wisdom.

We all know that we are not given perfect students to teach and easily love. God isn't done with them – or us – yet.

Suggested prayer: As school begins, we give You thanks, gracious God, for giving us the honor of assisting in shaping the lives of Your children. Grant us the wisdom, patience, and love to do it well. Amen.

Daily reminder: *When God began to create heaven and earth, there was a chaotic void.*

Righteousness: Genesis 6:5-22

"So the Lord said, 'I will blot out from the earth the human beings I have created ... for I am sorry that I have made them.' But Noah found favor in the sight of the Lord." (Genesis 6:7-8)

Does it ever seem that nothing you do makes a difference? According to some teacher training materials, if we only knew the right "trick," the belligerent, resistant students in our class would blossom into eager scholars. Example: Little Johnny hated to read until his teacher directed the class in *Hamlet*, and now he reads a different Shakespearean play every night. Yeah, right.

Let's face it: sometimes the ones we try the hardest with *don't* change. They hate to read when they come, and they hate to read when they leave. They don't understand why they need to know math when they have calculators. They see no purpose in studying history. They report weekly that their parents say teachers make too much money, can't hold real jobs, and can't control kids.

At least for the last comment, those parents are right. We can't "control" kids in the sense that we cannot turn them into exactly what we want them to be, no matter how hard or creatively we try. That power simply isn't ours, nor should it be. We can set an example, inspire, cajole, threaten, entertain, punish, applaud, and love our students sincerely and unconditionally, but ultimately, every individual is responsible for themselves and their own decisions.

Truth: Students sometimes choose to tune out, flunk out, or drop out. They sometimes choose to cheat, lie, and fight their way through life. We can analyze and sympathize, but if we have done our own jobs as well as we can, we cannot shoulder responsibility for their choices.

Only our own choices are within our control. Have we maintained faith in the value of education? Do we really love our students as God loves them, warts and all? Do we allow them the constant opportunity to change their choices? Do we present to them an example of righteous life and enthusiastic scholarship?

If you can always answer, "Yes" to all those questions, award yourself sainthood now. The rest of us are merely human. We sometimes give in to cynicism and hopelessness. But here's good news: We, too, can change at any point during our lives, during the day, even during fourth period algebra. All it takes is this realization: We do make a difference. Maybe not today. Maybe not this year. But at some point, every good thing you've done will matter to someone.

Look at Noah: God was ready to destroy life because of the wickedness of people (that God couldn't control!). But Noah maintained righteousness in the midst of universal evil. No matter where you teach, it can't be as bad as that! No doubt Noah sometimes thought he might as well join the faithlessness of those around him. But he didn't. And as a result, God gave us all another chance.

Suggested prayer: Gracious God, help me to remember that I cannot mold other people into what I want them to be. I can only ask that You mold me into the righteous person of Your will. Here I am. Amen.

Daily reminder: *But one person found favor in the eyes of the Lord.*

God In This Place: Genesis 28:10-22

"Then Jacob woke from his sleep and said, 'Surely the Lord is in this place – and I did not know it!'" (Genesis 28:16)

What is the holiest place you can think of? For me, it's the ocean. I can sit for hours watching the waves and listening to their power. The depth and mystery of the sea is my favorite image of God. Whenever I've been depressed or confused in my life, a trip to the ocean has been a sure restorative (Lake Michigan once had to do in a pinch). I've sung "How Great Thou Art" as loudly as I could with my toes in the Atlantic, Pacific, and Mediterranean.

For other people, holiness resides in mountains, museums, concert halls, cathedrals or simple churches. I know farmers who feel that way about their fields. Whatever place inspires it, the feeling is the same: Here, in this place with this view and this sound or silence, God's presence is palpable. You don't have to consciously pray in those circumstances; you just have to fully be there in order to commune with God.

Now consider this: Your classroom is holy. If the idea seems odd to you, remember that "holy" simply means "set apart." The connotation is usually that the area is set apart to the service of God, as in a church building. Yet a careful reading of the Bible teaches that holiness is not something we dedicate to God, but rather something that God grants to us, in many different places. Time and again, as in today's reading about Jacob, completely ordinary places become extraordinary by the revelation that "the Lord is in this place."

Now your classroom is obviously "set aside" to academics. In general, no other activity takes place there except teaching and learning (and the occasional party). High school classrooms are further dedicated to one particular subject; for example, my old room was decorated with literacy posters and shelves of books.

Now consider this: Why is your room set aside? Why has our society deemed it worthwhile to spend billions of dollars on specific places and people to educate our children in a vast public school system? Common to the many possible answers to that question is a concern for all children, regardless of socio-economic status or intellectual ability. We believe in the worth and potential of every child, and our schools are imperfect testament to that.

Now put that belief into terms of faith. Your classroom is a place set aside for the intellectual and social fulfillment of every child who walks through the door. The children don't need to do or pay anything to "deserve" it; we as a society offer it freely. Isn't that a form of grace? And what is the ultimate source of our service to each other if not our faith in the God who made each of us?

We cannot announce that our public school classroom is set aside to the service of God through service to each of God's children. But we can know it. And we can acknowledge it every time we walk through the door and remind ourselves that "the Lord is in this place."

Suggested prayer: Remind me constantly, God, to act in my classroom as I act in my church and every other holy place I sense Your presence. Amen.

Daily reminder: *Surely the Lord is in this place.*

Who Sent You? Genesis 45:1-15

"So it was not you who sent me here, but God; he has made me a father to Pharaoh, and lord of all his house and ruler over all the land of Egypt."
(Genesis 45:8)

I graduated from college many years ago with an accidental degree in English and no particular career plan. An advisor mentioned teaching as a possibility, and my answer was, "No way. I hate kids."

Funny how life works out. When people ask me now why I'm a teacher, I immediately think of the excellent teachers I've benefited from in my life. There is Ellen Davis, for example, my Hebrew professor in seminary. When I was the only student interested in third year study, the seminary cancelled the class, but we met weekly over coffee in her kitchen to read the prophets. It didn't even occur to me until later that she wasn't paid for her time. I would like to think that I have the same dedication to my subject and my students that she has. If I hadn't had such wonderful examples, would I be a teacher?

My career has also been shaped by a lack of options. My husband is a farmer and we live far out in the country with few opportunities for professional careers. If I had more choices, would I be a teacher?

Also, happy coincidences have shaped my career. At the same time I wanted to spend more time with our young children, a rare part-time opening occurred in my district. If that hadn't been available, would I still be a teacher? I don't know.

But perhaps the most honest answer for my motivations and development would be, simply, "God led me to where I am today."

This is how Joseph saw his life: a story that began in deep betrayal and ended in deep meaning and worth, shaped by God and not by men. Could he have saved Egypt and his own family if it hadn't been for all that had gone before? No. Three times in verses 5-8 Joseph repeats the truth that God has led him to the place of his life's meaning. He lifts his brothers from their guilt and shame, and sees the hand of God resting on them.

Who led you to the place you are now? Perhaps you had a worthy example in your life, or a persuasive advisor. Maybe you, like me, fell into teaching more by circumstance than by design, and have stayed there through serendipity.

No matter how you were led to a teaching life, if you find meaning and joy in your work, then the hand of God was guiding you more than you may have realized at the time. God does not manipulate our fates by tugging at puppet strings, but by placing people and opportunities in our lives, then urging us to choose and act with wisdom, faith, and love. The end result, if we have been paying attention, is to finally arrive at the place God has led us to all along.

Suggested prayer: Open my eyes, gracious God, so that I may recognize Your role in every event of my life. May I find joy in the midst of sorrow, peace in the midst of confusion, and You in every step of the way. Amen.

Daily reminder: *It is God who sent me here.*

Holy Ground: Exodus 3:1-12

"Remove the sandals from your feet, for the place on which you are standing is holy ground." (Exodus 3:5)

Moses encounters God in the course of his most mundane responsibility: tending sheep. The bush inhabited by the angel of the Lord was probably one he had passed by many times, thinking it to be just an ordinary plant (if he thought of it at all). On an ordinary day, in an ordinary place, during an ordinary chore, the totally extraordinary presented itself, and one of the turning points in history began.

Moses had options at that point. He could have seen the burning bush, shrugged his shoulders at the weirdness of it, and continued on his way. He could have ignored the voice with all manner of rationale. He did try arguing with God, but eventually gave in, which he didn't really have to do. He had a choice, and he chose to remove his sandals, listen, and obey.

The ground was holy not because of anything that had happened there, and indeed perhaps nothing important ever had. The ground was sacred because of communion with *who* was there. Moses' awareness of and response to God's calling made the moment and place of their meeting as holy as Mount Sinai was to become later. Our omnipresent God is everywhere in creation; the moments of our communion are, however, usually specific in time and place, and holy in every detail.

One of the sacred moments of my life, for example, happened between my home and a nearby small town, on a drive I make all the time. But one day my well-known world was transformed. I had officiated earlier that week at the funeral of a beloved teenage friend, and he was always on my mind. All of the sudden, from "no where," a voice clearly said, "It's true. God became one of us. It's all true."

I actually had to pull off the road, because I was shaking. I am an ordained minister and had preached the gospel for years, but never before had the utter truth of everything I said and believed been so clear and certain. Was an angel of the Lord speaking to me as I traveled a familiar road, making this world suddenly strange and wonderful? Was it my young friend, who now fully understood? Whatever the source, I've driven by that spot hundreds of times since, and I always recall that moment. No new messages have come to me there, but none need to.

Standing on holy ground doesn't change the terrain, but it changes the one standing. The voice of God breaks through in all sorts of places: sheep fields, country roads, city streets, homes, and churches.

And sometimes a hallway in a school, a table in a cafeteria, or a moment in a classroom may be a meeting place between the human and the divine. Approach it all with awe.

Suggested prayer: May I be mindful of Your constant presence in my life, O God, and open always to hearing Your voice and obeying Your commands. May I live on holy ground. Amen.
Daily reminder: *The place on which you are standing is holy ground.*

These People! Exodus 17:1-7

"What shall I do with this people? They are almost ready to stone me." (Exodus 17:4)

Let's be honest: There are days you wish you never became a teacher. It's not just your whining, lazy, arrogant, messed-up students. It's not just their pompous, ignorant parents. It's not just your cynical colleagues, or even your miracle-demanding principal. It's all these people!

When I have these (very rare) days, it helps to remind myself that no job is without challenges, and since teaching is so people-intensive, it stands to reason that people will usually be the challenge. It also helps to know that every now and then, *I* might be one of the people who is a challenge to someone else.

Before we talk about what to do on those days, let's review what not to do. As tempting as it may be, the teachers' lounge is not the place to vent about specific students, unpopular colleagues, the principal or the superintendent. We all know how the gossip game goes, and sooner or later your words (greatly twisted) will come back to haunt you. Yes, I speak from experience.

And although honesty is a great virtue, when you are angry, discouraged, or just plain tired, it is best to refrain from telling everyone exactly how you feel about them. New teachers will be surprised to know how long even the most difficult students will remember their hurt feelings; veteran teachers know it all too well.

So what should you do when the people you've been entrusted with are about to drive you crazy? Pity poor Moses.

Here was a great leader who had brought his people out of slavery in a strange land, and instead of thanks he got kvetching. In response, he showed us three perfect steps for days with difficult people:

(1) Talk to God. "Moses cried out to the Lord." We call that praying, and yes, you can do it at school. You can do it during class, even eye-to-eye with a child you'd like to throttle. But don't cry out. Just silently lift a passionate prayer, "God, help me. I don't know what to do with this kid!"

(2) Listen. "The Lord said to Moses…" You *will* receive an answer. You may not like it, and it may not make sense, but God will respond to your cry. In Moses' case, he was told to go strike a rock to get some water. In my case, 99% of the time the answer is, "Love them." Some days, I'd rather pound rocks.

(3) Do it. "Moses did so." He has by chapter 17 matured from the believer in chapter 3 who argued with God about directives. Now Moses just does what God tells him to do. This can happen to you, too.

By the way, I've had total turnarounds in my relationships with difficult students and colleagues. By loving them, of course.

Suggested prayer: What shall I do, O Lord, when I feel oppressed, unappreciated, or misunderstood? Remind me to always come to You, and then to live from You, my rock, my living water. Amen.

Daily reminder: *Cry out to the Lord, "What shall I do with these people?"*

Teach Them Well: Deuteronomy 11:13-28

"Teach them to your children, talking about them when you are at home and when you are away." (Deuteronomy 11:19)

Deuteronomy goes on to say believers should "write them [words of God] on the doorposts of your doors and on your gates." Devout Jews hang scrolls of Deuteronomy 6:4-9 and Deuteronomy 11:13-21 in little boxes on the doorposts of every room in their home (except bathrooms). These *mezuzot* are to remind them as they go about their daily business that they are to love and serve the Lord, and teach their children to do so.

I am not Jewish, but I have mezuzot on the two outer doors of our home. The scrolls simply read, "Love the Lord your God with all your heart, soul, and mind." One is in Hebrew and one in English; they were written not by a *sofer*, a special scribe, but by me. My Jewish friends may cringe at my unorthodoxy, but these doorpost reminders serve a holy purpose for me.

It is important to remember that loving and serving God entails a commandment to teach our children, to talk about divine matters at home and away. This is, of course, far more important than hanging scripture on your doorframes; it is also far more difficult when the children are not your own.

Do you teach the children in your classroom the love and service of God? Of course you cannot do so in words, but your every action, attitude, and utterance speak volumes. If students know you are a Christian, they may well judge all Christianity by how you act and what you say. Are you teaching them the joy and peace of faith, the fulfillment of service to God?

You may think you're teaching English, math, French, or the second grade. But we all know, though we are reluctant to admit it, that we teach far more. Some children look to their teachers as the only reliable adult role models in their lives. This should make you nervous.

Mezuzot serve a public purpose as much as a private one: they identify the homes they are posted in as Jewish (or as a Christian who stole a good idea). You can't nail up little boxes holding scripture on the doorframes of public classrooms, but you can include a small symbol of your faith in your workspace. I have a two-inch cross on my desk, and I admit that it sometimes gets lost amid the jumble of books and papers. Somehow, though, it always makes itself felt when I am grumpy or tired. At those times it seems to ask, "What are you teaching at this very moment?"

On my wall I have a tin ornament from Mexico, a hand pointing upward with a heart in the palm. It reminds me of the saying, "Hands to work, hearts to God," and always makes me smile (and work better?).

Think of something you could have in your room that would serve your faith in the same way: as a silent public witness and a private inspiration. We know we are to teach the children well, but sometimes we need to be reminded.

Suggested Prayer: Lord, may I live my life in such a way that I teach children of Your love and blessings without a word. Amen.

Daily reminder: *Teach love and blessing to your children.*

Choose: Joshua 24:14-22

"Now if you are unwilling to serve the Lord, choose this day whom you will serve … as for me and my household, we will serve the Lord." (Joshua 24:15)

There's really no such thing as an atheist. Everyone serves one god or another, though they may not call it by that name. Wealth, self, power, status, humanity, Earth, knowledge, sex, etc.: we can devote our lives, talents, and energies to all manner of false gods. The world has great power to lead us astray.

Because we're human, believers, too, can sometimes miss the mark. I speak from personal experience when I say even ordained ministers of the Word can serve the wrong purpose occasionally. For example, when I was in parish ministry I would too often worry about what the congregation would think about such and such, or how we were going to make ends meet, or when I was going to find time for *me.*

Teachers feel similar pressures. Am I pleasing the principal, the parents, the students, my colleagues, the Board of Education? Am I meeting state standards, NCLB, continuing education requirements? Am I meeting the specific intellectual and psychological needs of each child I encounter every day? Where am I on the pay scale, and when do I get a raise? How long until Christmas break!

In parish ministry or teaching ministry, the reality is the same: Such constant worries blind us to the truth and joy of each moment; they blind us to God. I finally realized that the devil will swallow a seed of caring and concern to grow a weed patch of worry and doubt. A choice is set up in our minds: Success or peace? How often do we choose the elusive race for success? What does "success" even mean? If you make everyone happy this week, that doesn't mean you won't have the same issues next week! The obsession with being "good" as defined by other people, standards, and monetary measures, is a false god.

Of course being good isn't bad. Exceptional teachers are always sensitive to those around them, and we always strive to do our best. But Christians don't live to serve our bosses, professors, or any institution. We aren't even here "for the children" (gasp!). We serve no one but God.

The funny thing is that when we devote our every breath and thought to God, the rest becomes easy. I know the difference it makes in my day when I haven't taken the time to commune with my Creator in the morning. My students know it, too, and so do my colleagues. Peace of mind and spirit will carry us through anything.

We aren't tempted by the gods of the Amorites, Perizzites, Canaanites, Hittites, Girgashites, and Hivites like the people of Joshua's day were. But tempted we are indeed by a pantheon of noble purposes and appearances. Only one of them will set your soul at rest. Choose.

Suggested prayer: I place nothing above or before You, gracious God. Bless my choice, keep it sure. Amen.
Daily reminder: *As for me, I will serve the Lord.*

Listening: 1 Samuel 3:1-19

"Now the Lord came and stood there, calling as before, 'Samuel! Samuel!' And Samuel said, 'Speak, for your servant is listening.'" (1 Samuel 3:10)

Samuel doubtless learned much under the wise prophet Eli, but listening was the most important skill. In today's passage, the Lord called to Samuel three times, but the child did not recognize God's voice, because "the word of the Lord had not yet been revealed to him." It is his teacher who finally realizes who the voice belongs to. Eli knows this without hearing the Lord's call himself; his insight comes from knowing God, and from knowing Samuel.

Our students may not hear such dramatic calls from God, but they will be called unto. Will they recognize the voice? Will they heed it? Who is their teacher to help them discern their path?

Maybe you think, "Oh, I teach algebra, this doesn't apply to me." Let me tell you a story. Sometimes by lucky chance I have the same students for three years in a row. This happened with a lovely young woman named Alicia. She set me straight on the first day of her sophomore year: "My parents don't care about my grades, so don't nag me about them. They don't matter." By her senior year she was a straight-A student taking college level math and writing classes. She went on to college on academic and sports scholarships.

What happened? I taught that college writing class, and my students once had to write about a turning point in their lives. Here is what Alicia wrote:

"I used to be a poor student because I just didn't care. Then in the 10th grade Mr. Wright, my math teacher, took me aside and asked me why I was having trouble with our assignments. I told him I didn't have a problem, I just didn't care enough to do the work. He said, 'Alicia, you're too smart to have that kind of attitude. Don't waste yourself.' No one had ever called me smart before. I wondered if he was right, so I thought I'd try a little harder just to see. All my grades improved, and I realized that I really am smart after all."

Her paper went on to say that her new confidence and determination were problems in her family; her father especially seemed threatened by a daughter who was quickly becoming a new self. He was very upset when she was accepted to college, because he didn't think "poor Mexican girls" needed higher education, but by then Alicia knew herself well enough to lead her own life.

That math teacher is a devoted Christian. With Alicia's permission, I showed him her essay. His eyes teared up and he said, "I had no idea."

That's the point. When we lead students to listen to the positive voices crying out to them, we don't know how it will affect their lives. But if the voice is of God, we have done a mighty work.

Suggested prayer: My students hear so many voices urging them to do and be many things, dear God. May I help reveal Your word to them. Amen.

Daily Reminder: *Speak, O Lord, I am listening.*

In The Name Of The Lord: 1 Samuel 17:31-51

"You come to me with sword and spear and javelin; but I come to you in the name of the Lord." (1 Samuel 17:45)

The story of David and Goliath is often used to illustrate the ability of the little guy to successfully take on the big guy, as in consumers versus big business, or private citizens overcoming big government. But a careful reading of the story shows that David isn't the one who defeated the giant Philistine. Instead, he defeated Goliath because he came not clothed in armor with mighty weapons, but in the name of the Lord.

This Biblical story reminds me of one of my favorite moments in secular literature. In J.R.R. Tolkein's *The Fellowship of the Ring*, the ancient wizard Gandalf confronts the evil powers of the abyss with this wonderful warning: "I am a servant of the Secret Fire … You cannot pass. The dark fire will not avail you … Go back to the Shadow!" Clearly, Gandalf's wisdom and power are not self-generated, but are rooted in a strength transcending reality. Sacrificing himself, Gandalf seems to be defeated, but he later rises triumphant.

We hold dual strengths in Godly confrontations with Goliaths and the abyss. Clearly, the eyes of faith do not look upon any adversary or adversity as ultimately victorious, no matter what happens in the short term. Even death is defeated by faith, so what is there to fear? Any enemy that shakes its fist at us is bound to be weaker and less significant than our God. And if God is for us, who can be against us?

More important than how we feel about threatening giants, however, is how we feel about ourselves. I like to think of myself as a servant of the Secret Fire, too; in my case, that would be the Holy Spirit. I have often confronted difficult situations and people with a whispered assurance to myself, "I come in the name of the Lord," or with an image of the Dove descending to me in a tongue of flame. It makes me stand a little taller.

Realizing that we are not alone in our battles, whatever they may be, adds a depth of joy to our daily struggles that children of the world never know. Maybe we aren't tackling giant warriors or demons from hell, but the forces of evil come in many more subtle guises. Do we only cringe at injustice, oppression, and harassment in our schools? Do we ignore blatant dishonesty, cynicism, and hate in our classrooms, the teachers' lounge, or the playing field? Or do we confront everything that would destroy God's will with the assurance that the mighty kingdom is within us at this moment?

A word of caution: I have lost my temper when overwhelmed by injustice or even unkindness. I pray daily for patience to make sure that my "righteous anger" doesn't turn into a Goliath of its own. We need to carefully aim our little stones.

Maybe the story shouldn't be called "David and Goliath"; maybe we should call it "David and the Lord." But then, that would give away the ending.

Suggested prayer: Gracious God, envelop me not with heavy armor nor massive weapons, but with Your Spirit, ready in love and courage to defeat all that is not You. Amen.

Daily reminder: *I come in the name of the Lord.*

An Understanding Mind: 1 Kings 3:5-14

"Give your servant therefore an understanding mind to govern your people, able to discern between good and evil ..." (1 Kings 3:9)

I consider this one of the most beautiful passages in the Bible. Solomon is a hero to emulate not because he was rich and powerful, but because above all else he sought wisdom. When I was a child, he was the Old Testament character I wanted to be. Now I am a mature woman, and I still want an understanding mind, especially to teach God's people. What does that mean for our lives?

There are, of course, many things that teachers need to understand. Most of us have taken batteries of tests to assure employers that we understand our subjects and basic pedagogy. We strive to understand each of our students and their unique strengths and needs. Maybe we even want to understand education policy on state and federal levels, but that's a whole other book!

In each of these cases, teachers are called upon to understand people and facts outside themselves. Solomon was asking for something far more difficult: he wanted an understanding of the world and its people that arose from an internal discernment of good and evil. He was, in other words, asking God to show him the path to follow in any life situation, so that he could then lead God's people in righteousness.

The wisdom of Solomon doesn't show up on Praxis tests or in job interviews. But students will test us daily, and we only pass with God's help.

Most teenagers, for example, have a strong sense of justice, but they don't always know how to act on it. Once, a high school junior, a popular athlete, wrote a violently obscene poem about a young woman in our class and passed it around his buddies as a "joke." I suffered internal combustion when I found it, then got even madder when the boy's parents defended him and he was given minimum discipline. Oh, hell hath no fury like I had.

When I got home that day, I got on my knees and prayed for guidance. The next day, our planned lesson was suspended in favor of a calmly delivered survey and impromptu lesson on the limits of free speech. Each student in the class answered questions about, frankly, good and evil, though I hadn't worded it that way. I then showed the anonymous results to the class on an overhead projector, and we respectfully discussed them. The overwhelming conclusion was that the boy's classmates strongly disapproved of what he had done, but they didn't know how to respond to him. He learned far more from that lesson indirectly taught by his peers than from a one-day suspension and my righteous anger. Incidentally, the girl involved in the incident thanked me profusely in private.

A lesson that day for me was the answer to: "Should teachers ignore conversations and notes among students in their class?" Every girl said, "No. Teachers need to know what's going on all the time." It was my wake-up call that students need and want governance in the classroom. They know what's good and what is not, but they need someone to lead them in action. That would be, with the help of God, us.

Suggested prayer: Gracious God, I have the burden and joy of teaching life. Give me a discerning mind to lead my students in paths of righteousness. Amen.

Daily reminder: *Give to me an understanding mind.*

What Are You Doing Here? 1 Kings 19:1-18

"...and after the fire a sound of sheer silence. ... Then there came a voice to him that said, 'What are you doing here, Elijah?'" (1 Kings 19:12-13)

We can discern the voice of God in all of nature, most impressively the roar of ocean tide and the majesty of thunder. But as Elijah learned, sometimes we need to listen instead to "a sound of sheer silence."

It is, of course, much easier to pay attention to loud, dramatic sounds. In our day, silence is actually hard to come by. If you live in a city, chances are there are constant background noises in your life, many of which are mechanical. The voice of the Lord is not in those. For Elijah, the city's voices meant fearful threats, and he escaped into the wilderness, eventually into a mountain cave. There, finally, he listened not to the voice of the hate-filled queen of that world, but to the King of all worlds.

"What are you doing here, Elijah?" God asks, twice. Each time Elijah answers indirectly, because he is in fact not doing anything but running from his fears. The forces of death, at that point, control his life.

Because Elijah could not give a good answer the first time, God grabs his attention through a display of mighty forces of nature, then brings a deep calm so that Elijah can really listen. Again, Elijah tells God he is running from death threats. This time, God tells him what he needs to do instead, and it includes returning to the fray. Elijah obeys, and there is no more mention of his fears.

When did you last answer the question, "What are you doing here?" Maybe on your worst days in class you say that to yourself as a weak joke, but what are you *really* doing in that room, with those people, holding that book?

Teachers enter our profession for various reasons, not all of them good. I had a science teacher in high school who had flunked out of medical school, and he was mightily bitter (and, of course, a terrible teacher). I had an economics professor in college who definitely knew her subject, but absolutely hated students. She was finally taken out of the classroom and made an assistant dean, where she couldn't bother anyone.

They aren't the only people who approach their classrooms as a sort of cave where they hide from the disappointments and demands of the world, or as a little kingdom that they rule for the love of power, not love of the ruled. They aren't where they should be, they aren't doing what they should do, and none of this is God's will for their lives. It goes without saying that they are unhappy, unfulfilled people.

Try a little experiment this week to make sure you're where you're supposed to be: When you first get to school, sit in your car an extra few minutes and sincerely ask yourself, "What am I doing here?" Then listen not to traffic, the ringing of bells, or the shouts of students, but to the voice of the Lord telling you what you are to do, that day in that place. I don't know what your answer will be. But obey it. By the end of the week, you will be confident in your calling.

Suggested prayer: God, there is so much noise in my life and in my head. Open my mind and soul to hear Your voice speaking in sheer silence, leading me to the place I need to go and showing me what I am to do there. In thanksgiving, Amen.

Daily reminder: *I am here to do the work of the Lord.*

Reading From The Book: Nehemiah 8:1-12

"So they read from the book, from the law of God, with interpretation. They gave the sense, so that the people understood the reading."
(Nehemiah 8:8)

Ours is a bookish house. Bookshelves overflow our library into halls and staircases, and a mountain of books is dangerously stacked on my headboard. I even have a tall case of cookbooks in our kitchen, and I'm a terrible cook. I love books.

One of my seniors once described me this way: "Ms. Mathieu has this thing about books. If you come into her room and say you need something good to read, she'll stop whatever she's doing and go nuts until she gets the perfect thing for you."

Luckily I married a man with the same passion for reading, so he never complains about my literary purchases. Like most teachers, I spend hundreds every year out of pocket for my classroom, which has an overflowing bookcase of freebies. I pick them up at yard sales and Goodwill, and then give them away to my students, some of whom act like they've never owned a book. ("You mean I can keep it? It's mine? Really?") Maybe they haven't. What I really love is finding something perfect for a particular student, then coming in the next day and handing it to them, saying, "I went book shopping again this weekend and found this. Thought you'd like it." If it's a student I've had problems with, the problems are over. Books are like that.

Of course, I don't collect just any books, whether to keep or give away. There's too much power in the printed word to take it lightly. If I haven't read the book myself, I have to trust the author, a reviewer, or a recommendation before I'll trust the books to my students. What will the message of the book do for their spirits? I don't mean books have to be squeaky clean with happy endings. Such books are often quite dull, actually. Life is full of corruption and pain, and students know it, sometimes first hand. They appreciate books that acknowledge temptation and sorrow, but then lift the protagonist out of danger. They look to books as guides in life, and they have concerns and curiosity plenty.

For example, one student in my Hispanic literature class wrote this on his first semester evaluation: "I feel more importantly these books have helped me to understand how people think and will react in certain situations." He is approaching the answer I give when students ask me why I love books so much: "Because I love life, and that's what they're about."

If you are in a public school that teaches the ultimate book, the Bible, as literature or cultural icon, then you have my blessing and a tinge of envy. Most of us do not have that freedom. But we have power. Every book that is opened by a student has the potential to change their lives, for better or worse. What do you choose to share with your students, either as a class or individually? Do you have a ready list of suggestions when they come to you with questions and problems? Do you impart a deep understanding of a righteous life by the books you open to and with them? If so, rejoice. If not, start reading.

Suggested prayer: May the books I read to, with, and for my students be a cause of understanding and rejoicing for the life You intend for us all. Amen.

Daily reminder: *Open the book and teach understanding.*

Hard Times: Job 1:13-2:10

"Shall we receive the good at the hand of God, and not receive the bad?" (Job 2:10)

You never know what will happen in life. Your house might burn down, you might lose your job, your marriage may fall apart, your children may be imprisoned by addiction, obsession, or judicial authorities. No one has perfect health. Without a doubt, people you love are going to die, as you will, but we don't know when, where, or how.

When tragedy strikes, will you curse God? Worse yet, will you cease to believe? If so, then you curse or disbelieve in a Santa Claus God: the popular concept of God as a superpower who gives you everything you want. You make a list: good health, secure job, lots of money, love unfailingly returned, students who always behave and are eager to learn, etc. And God better deliver!

That isn't our God. The Divine is, however, in tune to our deepest needs. I haven't actually cursed God, but I have yelled heavenward good and loud. When I was a kid, we moved a lot. In junior high, which is bad enough for anyone, we moved to a small Southern town. I hated it. I was a liberal Yankee who had never experienced segregation, and I got beat up for being a "n– lover." My older sisters were grown and gone. I had no friends and no prospect of making any. I didn't even have a dog.

So I did what any good little Christian girl should do: I went to the empty lot next to our house and screamed at God. "Just one friend!" I yelled to the heavens. "Is that too much? Just one!" Many years later, I can still feel the pain in my voice and in my heart that day. Adolescent loneliness is a terrible thing.

The next day, honestly, a new kid was on my bus, a girl from California, which is even worse than being a Yankee. Another misfit. We became instant best friends. My thank you prayer was short: At 13, I wasn't at all surprised to get what I needed.

I haven't yelled at God since, but I haven't taken friends for granted, either. Partly as a result of that dramatic experience, I see all goodness in life, from friends to my own children, a wonderful husband, a job I love, and so much more, as gifts from God. It isn't that I deserve it in any way, and I know I could lose it all at any moment. That's what makes every moment of life precious. When the worst – death –has come to those I love, I thank God over and over for my love and their life. I disagree with Job: Nothing is ever taken – it has all been given.

There's a follow up to my junior high experience. Recently I was shopping at a seacoast resort in Massachusetts with my sister, and the young clerk had a thick Southern accent, very out of place there. I asked her where she was from, and to my amazement, she said the same small town I had hated so much. "I went to school there years ago," I managed to say. "My father's the principal!" she cheerfully replied. I couldn't get out of the store fast enough. But later I looked up my old school's web site. Imagine my delight to find that it's now fully integrated, with an active multicultural club and a dynamic student body. It didn't look like the same place at all.

No, you never do know what will happen in life.

Suggested prayer: Through blessings and challenges, joy and sorrow, may I always live conscious of Your embrace, Lord of my life. Amen.
Daily reminder: *God holds me this day.*

The Words Of My Heart: Psalm 19

"Let the words of my mouth and the meditation of my heart be acceptable to you, O Lord, my rock and my redeemer." (Psalm 19:14)

A student once wrote on my class evaluation, "I like this class because you make me feel really smart, not like Mr. Brown who tells me I'm just filtering air." I want to believe that Mr. Brown mistakenly thought he was witty, but chances are better that the teacher was at the end of his rope, and his true feelings fell out of his mouth.

I can't be too hard on Mr. Brown, because I suffer from a bad case of sharp tongue myself. In my case, that tongue gets bitten a lot, but the words are still there, in my mind and in my heart. I don't like how my colleague speaks to students, but I understand him.

Whenever I preach, I begin the sermon by praying Psalm 19:14. Words spoken (or written) in interpretation and sharing of the Word need to be carefully chosen. A great deal of thought goes into my preaching and writing. I would never dream of being rude or insulting to a congregation or reader.

So why am I sometimes tempted to be sharp and cruel to kids? If you've taught more than a week, you know what I mean. The fidgets who won't sit still, the socialites who won't stop talking, the excuse-makers who never get their work done, the cools who stroll into class late every day, the you-can't-make-me toughs that you know never learned to read but they dodge the issue quite well and maddeningly. The list goes on. For those and others, there are comments on the tip of my tongue that don't make it out, but they're still there more often than I'd like them to be.

If you don't say it, does it matter that you think it? Yes, yes, yes.

For one thing, students pick up on far more than we give them credit for. The way you look at them, the way you don't look at them, your tone of voice, your eye contact, etc. If you're thinking it, you don't have to say it. It's there.

Secondly, if you're thinking of how they drive you nuts, even for that split second, you aren't thinking of a way to love and help them. I once had a colleague who did nothing but complain about a certain student. I finally said, "So how are you teaching her?" Within a few weeks, she bragged about the great progress the same student had made. Perhaps it was the teacher who started thinking differently first.

Thirdly, and most importantly, God knows everything you think. Scary, isn't it? I want to get to a point in my life where not just every word and action, but every "meditation of my heart" really is acceptable to God. I have a way to go, but I'm working on it.

The stunning first four verses of Psalm 19 are an inspiration toward this goal. Consider the heavens, which do not speak at all, yet "their voice goes out through all the earth." This is communication not from saying but from being. That's what I want. I don't want to just filter air; I want to be God's breath. I'm going to start silently praying my sermon opening at the start of every class.

Suggested prayer: May the words of my mouth and the meditation of my heart be acceptable to You, O Lord. Amen.
Daily reminder: *Lift every thought to God.*

What You Don't Know: Psalm 139:1-18

"O Lord, you have searched me and known me." (Psalm 139:1)

How many times have you heard colleagues characterize students this way:

"That Smith kid, all he cares about is football."

"You know Susie? The one who's always thinking about boys?"

"That kid is so lazy. I bet all he does on the weekends is sleep and watch TV."

Maybe, God forbid, you've said something like that yourself. But after years of teaching, if it's one thing I know, it's that I don't know. Just when you have students all figured out, they can really surprise you.

Sometimes the surprises are sad. Like when a sweet, quiet little guy writes, "… but then my dad became an alcoholic, and my mom divorced him. I still miss him." Or when the young woman who's never caught up with work suddenly moves because her dad found her and her mom again. We have no idea of the sadness and fear some of our students live with.

And sometimes the surprises are good. Like when the big tough jock breaks into song in your class, and yeah, it's disruptive, but you're so amazed by his beautiful voice that you applaud along with everyone else when he bows. Or a girl who barely knows English works extra hard on an assignment, and her deeply felt essay brings tears to your eyes.

Or there was the struggling reader I had one year who, when it came time to memorize a soliloquy from Shakespeare, couldn't make up his mind, so he memorized two. Then he acted them out in the middle of the room, and I dared not breathe, he was so good. That was years ago, and I still get goose bumps remembering it.

I could go on, but you get the point. It's hard to fully know the people we live with every day or the friends we've had for life, let alone students we have for only a year or two. In one small school I had the same students three years in a row, and I would have said I knew them well. But upon graduation a rather "lazy class clown" joined the Army and volunteered to fight in Iraq because he believed strongly in America's mission there. It was the last thing on Earth I expected from him.

There's a great danger in thinking we know everything about our students, including what they're capable of and where they're going in life. In extremis, we lock them into very small boxes, or take their talents for granted. They don't see their own potential, and the work it takes to fulfill it, because no one around them does, either. Or we blame them for faults when we have no understanding of the roots of those problems and how they might be helped.

There is, on the flip side, a great joy in admitting we don't know them completely and don't presume to. It leaves the door of possibilities wide open, with each year – no, each day – given as an opportunity for renewal and resurrection.

We can't truly know our students, and that knowledge should keep us humble in our service to them. God knows them, and we know God, and that's all that matters.

Suggested prayer: Remind me daily, God, that You have a will for each of my students. Keep my mind and heart open to their life in You. Amen.

Daily reminder: *God knows us all.*

Wisdom: Proverbs 8

"For wisdom is better than jewels, and all that you may desire cannot compare with her." (Proverbs 8:11)

My son was very impressed with a classmate who could list all 50 states in alphabetical order *and* name their capitols.

"She must like geography," I said.

"Oh no," he corrected. "She's just really smart."

We had a discussion about whether memorization of facts really constitutes "smart," but I quickly gave up. If he wants to admire his friend, that's okay.

Maybe I was a little jealous of her. I, too, used to know all the state capitols, but in that discussion with my son, I couldn't think of more than ten. It's kind of sad.

But even though I'm no longer "smart" in the 10-year-old sense, I feel I'm gaining wisdom every year. What's the difference?

In the Bible, Wisdom is an eternal living attribute of God. She was present at the foundation of the world, not only helping God, but rejoicing and delighting in His work. Wisdom is the life force of faith. The absence of Wisdom is not ignorance: It is death.

The death in verse 36 isn't a physical cessation of function; instead it is a morbidity of soul that can easily be present in walking, talking, breathing people. Conversely, when Wisdom says, "Whoever finds me finds life," she means not animation, but the eternal spiritual life in God that was manifested and offered in the life, death, and resurrection of Jesus Christ. Wise people seek, find, and treasure God's *Logos*: plan, Word, logic, Wisdom.

Alzheimer's disease runs in my family, and this gives me pause every time another fact gets lost in my crowded brain. But I take heart from my mother's last days, when she actually became more loving than she'd been before the disease wasted her mind. It was as if the defenses that made her a rather cold person collapsed, and a sweet child-like trust replaced them. She was less and less smart, and more and more wise.

I used to pride myself on my IQ when I was young, but now it just doesn't matter. Now I am far more interested in how I treat people, and in the development of my spirit. That's Wisdom speaking.

We all have smart students in our classrooms, and we have wise ones, too, and they aren't always the same. Our educational system does not recognize wise spirits or loving hearts, and that's a shame. We do acknowledge types of intelligence, but students aren't often led to discover those strengths within themselves.

Years ago I asked an older friend, one of the saints of our small town, what he would change if he could live his life over. He immediately answered, "I'd go to college so I could be smarter." I laughed out loud. "A lot of idiots graduate from college," I said. "You're smarter than a lot of people I know with Ph.D.'s."

We were, of course, talking about different kinds of smart: the facts and theories the world respects, and the Wisdom of life and love that is God. They're not the same.

Suggested prayer: May I share with my students Your wisdom, not by what I know, but by what I do and whose I am. Amen.
Daily reminder: *Wisdom is more precious than jewels.*

What's The Point? Ecclesiastes 4:1-8

"For whom am I toiling,' they ask, 'and depriving myself of plea-sure?'" (Ecclesiastes 4:8)

What would you do if you won a million dollars?

I'd put aside some for my children, give some to my church and favorite charities, and invest another chunk for a travel fund. I'd set up a grant foundation for the rest.

And I'd keep teaching.

We all have colleagues who aren't teaching so much as wait-ing for retirement, or for something "better," like their admin-istrative license. They can't wait to get out of the classroom. Years of teaching have convinced them that there's no point in trying to educate the little boogers. They really want to do something else from 8-to-4, like make more money or just relax. I feel sorry for those people.

From time to time I am asked to become a principal, but I'm pretty sure I'd hate it. For one thing, I don't do well on commit-tees because I'm so bossy. And frankly, I like summers off.

But the real reason I don't move into an office is that I love my students, even when they're ornery. I once sent two teen-age boys to the office for fighting, and after I wrote the referral, I said, "You may find this hard to believe right now, but I really like both of you. But you need to grow up!" And one of them sheepishly said, "Yeah, we know."

They know all about us. The other day I overheard two stu-dents talking about a teacher. "I don't think he likes me," one said.

"Don't worry," said his friend. "He doesn't like anybody."

The first boy laughed. "You're right. I feel better."

Now that teacher really should ask himself, "For whom am I toiling and depriving myself of pleasure?" If he's miserable and can't stand students, then there is no good reason for him to be teaching.

Even if he's the sole breadwinner for his ailing wife and ten children (he's not), he needs to find another line of work. No one should work only for the sake of a paycheck, least of all teachers. Even if he's some certified genius in his field of study (he's not), he needs to be doing something else. No one should teach just so they can pontificate from a podium to a captive audience.

So if we aren't teaching just for the sake of our pay or a chance to show off, then why are we?

Ecclesiastes has the question right. It isn't "why" we toil, but "for whom." The answer surely includes the grocer, tailor, and landlord to whom we owe compensation. And we can truthfully say we work for our students or the betterment of society. But even far beyond that, all Christian toil tends the vineyards of God.

If we work for material gain or worldly recognition, then our toil is indeed in vain. But if we act in response to God's grace through service to and love for His children, then our reward will be great: Our deepest spirits will be content with a job well done, and for holy reasons.

Suggested prayer: Remind me daily, God, that I toil for You, and there is no greater pleasure. Amen.
Daily reminder: *I work for God as my living.*

Keeping The Vineyard: Isaiah 27:2-5

"A pleasant vineyard, sing about it! I, the Lord, am its keeper; every moment I water it." (Isaiah 27:2-3)

Jesus described the building of the kingdom of God in terms of such humble tasks as tending flocks, casting nets, kneading dough, sowing seed, and building houses.

Another common analogy, reflected in today's scripture reading, is that of tending vineyards, from the planting to harvesting of grapes. Among the oldest cultivated plants known, grapes are relatively easy to take care of. In the right soil, their roots, which can extend up to 40 feet, will find what they need. However, the vines do need to be carefully planted and then conscientiously pruned for productivity.

The meaning for our lives is clear. When God tends the vineyard, we are the grapevines. When we are rooted by and in God, we are able to dig deep and find what we need; indeed, the Lord waters us daily. It does not matter what kind of soil we are planted in; our needs will be met, and we will thrive. If an evil weed intertwines itself in our lives, God will "march to battle against it," keeping us safe from harm.

The analogy also applies when we toil in the vineyard not as vines that grow, but as farmers working toward a bountiful harvest. As a shepherd tends sheep, we tend young and vulnerable plants until they are established enough to sustain themselves.

My husband is a wheat farmer, and I know that planting and harvesting are the most critical times of the growing cycle. We are also constantly on the watch for weeds and pests, and pluck them out as soon as possible. Our fields produce the staff of life for many people, and we take our responsibility seriously.

Now switch the image from tender vines and stalks to the children in your classrooms. They are, indeed, like young plants, and they have been set in some very rocky soil. Some of them are scorched, some are wilting, others are drowning. Too many of them are being slowly choked by the weeds of dysfunctional families and a powerful culture of sex, violence, and instant gratification.

What can their roots tap into? They need to understand that life has purpose, meaning, and hope; they must develop an inner strength to see them through hard times. You teach a subject, yes, but more importantly, you teach the goodness of life that they may not learn to trust anywhere else.

Who waters them daily? I'm the "grandma" type, and tough teenage boys will suddenly give me a hug, then walk away without a word. You, too, may be the rare adult who gives your students love and attention. Their spirits die without it.

Who goes to battle for them? Kids can't always stand up for or protect themselves. You must be willing to advocate for them, not only in their education, but also in other areas of need in their lives. You aren't taking on extra roles when you fight for your students: you're being a Christian, and that's all you need to be.

In time, the best grapes are made into wine, even for the Lord's supper. We can pray for no better harvest.

Suggested prayer: Gracious God, you have given me an awful responsibility: to do the same work You do in the world. Be with me every step of the way. Amen.

Daily reminder: *Every moment I water it.*

Temptations: Matthew 4:1-11

"Away with you, Satan!" (Matthew 4:10)

Temptation! There's an endless subject. "Lead me not into temptation," the joke goes, "because I can find it myself." Can't we all?

For example, I am one of the millions of Americans considered obese, and I am determined to eat well and reach a healthy weight. A simple trip to the grocery store is laden with danger. Of course food is a gift from God, necessary for life. But when we misuse it, as in gluttony and waste, it becomes a means of sin.

In today's passage, Jesus refuses to turn stones into bread. Of course he didn't disapprove of bread; he later shared it as a symbol of his own body. Satan's temptation was to put physical eating above and before nourishment by God, and Jesus knew better.

Gluttony has obvious results, but we daily face many more subtle temptations. Teachers can have their own little kingdoms in their classrooms, and we've all seen colleagues abuse their power. We may all be tempted to say what we think at all times, but such honesty could seriously harm the spirit of a child, and in that case, it becomes sin. We may be tempted to let the rules slide with this one but not that one, because he "deserves" punishment, but our favorites don't. That's when flexibility becomes sin.

"Because I said so" can be sin. I was one of those annoying, "But why?" kids, and my exasperated parents frequently gave me that maddening answer. Imagine my surprise when I heard myself saying, "Because I said so" to my own kids! But teachers, like parents, owe children a good reason for everything we require them to do. Authority is necessary, but without constant self-checks, it is easily abused.

Then there are the temptations to lead an easy life, away from all struggle and strife. Some people cocoon their lives and cushion their minds with alcohol, drugs, or material wealth. Religion can have the same effect if we think of ourselves as better than "they" are and ignore or belittle the world's pain. Faith becomes sin when it leads us to cease loving the world as it is, here and now.

Satan offered Jesus the world, and Jesus refused, not because he didn't love the world, but because he loved God more. That's what our own choices come down to as well. The evil that we pray to be delivered from isn't some hideous monster. It's instead very seductive, very tempting. If I were to make a movie of Jesus' life, I'd have the best-looking, smoothest-talking actor I could find play Satan.

Maybe I'd figure out a way to put a schoolteacher in my movie. Satan could whisper in her ear, "I'll make them all quiet and studious if you'll just dance with me," and lovely music will be playing as she looks into his big blue eyes. Then she'll remember stones into bread, and she knows, just in the nick of time, that he's about to make God's own children into something they're not. She wants them to exercise free will, even if that means messy moments in her own life. "Sorry," she tells him, "I can't dance right now; I've got to teach." And she shuts the door in his face. What a scene!

I'll need to lose a few more pounds before I can play it.

Suggested prayer: Thank you, God, for giving me the gift of choosing who I am, what I say, and what I do. May all my choices be pleasing in Your sight. Amen.

Daily reminder: *Choose God.*

Watch The Heavens Open: Mark 1:1-11

"... he saw the heavens torn apart and the Spirit descending like a dove on him. And a voice came from heaven, 'You are my Son, the Beloved.'" (Mark 1:10-11)

Medieval monks who made a specialty of caring for lepers would greet these disfigured pariahs with the words, "Ah, Christ! It is you again."

What a wonderful attitude toward others, and one that we could learn much from. We may not have lepers in our schools, but we all know students who are outcasts and misfits. We all have students in our classes that, frankly, we'd prefer to be somewhere else. You know what I mean: You can't help but smile on the days they're absent.

God does not intend them or us to be that way. Perhaps your class lepers are ignorant of God's grace or have even rejected it. But you haven't.

Because it's true of any random group of people, I know that not all of the lepers who came to the monks were nice people; they probably weren't even all grateful. They were there out of desperation. But the monks who received the lepers were not randomly chosen; they were there for a purpose and a calling, and so every supplicant was greeted with an attitude of holy reverence. I cannot help but think that even the most hardened visitor would have eventually known himself blessed to be there.

Now you can't greet your students at a public school with the words, "Ah Christ, it's you again." But how do you greet them? At my last high school, students changed classes every 54 minutes. Our principal wanted teachers in the hall during passing times for security reasons. I was annoyed at this initially, because I always had work to do in my room. But I turned it into an opportunity to greet each student by name with a smile as they came through my door. We all know to do that on the first day of school, but I've been surprised what a difference constant welcoming makes.

And when that leper comes down the hall, I imagine the heavens opening on him.

In the passage from Mark, it seems that only Jesus himself saw the heavens open and the dove descend. Did others hear the voice, too? It doesn't say. In the parallel text in John 1, the Baptizer says he saw the Spirit descend on Jesus, but it doesn't say anything about the voice from heaven.

Baptism is an outward sign of inward grace, simultaneously a public and private act. No person creates anything new in the act of baptism; instead both the baptized and witnesses acknowledge a given truth. It is an act of reception, not force. Witnesses may experience one truth while the baptized has an awakening of their own. The public nature of the sacrament invites multiple perspectives.

No, you cannot throw water on your students and baptize them in the hall, so don't even think of it. But you can extend to them the grace that has been given to you. Imagine that they have accepted God's blessing. As they walk down the hall to your door, imagine the heavens opening just for them. Here is the Spirit, and hear the voice. It's what you really want for them, isn't it?

Maybe they aren't Christ, yet. But you are.

Suggested prayer: God, You commanded me to love. May I learn to see all of my students through Your eyes, and speak to them with Your voice. Amen.

Daily reminder: *Watch the heavens open.*

Rocky Ground: Mark 4:1-9

"Other seed fell into good soil and brought forth grain." (Mark 4:8)

At some point, teachers need to recognize their limits. We sow the seed, we cultivate the fields, but we have no choice as to the ground we till.

There are so many rocks and thorns out there.

I think of the student who plans to drop out so she can support her unplanned but not unwelcome baby. Or the children who live on the street, in their cars, or in drug- and violence-infested neighborhoods. What about the kindergartner who describes the most significant man in her life as "the man who sleeps with Mommy?" The third grader who must decide between divorcing parents? The high school student who shuffles between relatives because, as they will loudly tell you, no one wants him? Unless you live somewhere I've never heard of, you can add your own examples. These children may come to school as a safe place, but they live on rocky ground.

Children in stable, loving homes abundant in life's necessities are still at risk from the thorns of our culture: drugs, alcohol, promiscuity, materialism, violence, and apathy as a lifestyle. Their souls and minds are so easily choked.

What's a teacher to do? We can't police the morals of students, let alone their parents, we can't guarantee everyone meaningful work at appropriate pay, we can't fix dysfunctional families, we can't put a force field around our students to protect them from all of life's temptations and evils. Sometimes we feel like we can't do anything.

But the value is not in choosing the ground. The value is in sowing the seed.

I stayed on the ninth floor of a hotel recently in a large city. The balcony was made of concrete and steel, rocky ground if there ever was any. And yet, on the edge of that balcony, a flower was growing. Where had the seed come from, so high up in such an inhospitable setting? Maybe the wind, maybe a passing bird. Perhaps many such seeds had fallen there, but this one, for reasons that can't be known, was the only one that dug in and yielded a harvest: a little fuzzy purple flower busting out of the concrete. "Here's a sermon!" I thought.

If directions had been given to "go grow a flower in the concrete," the workers would surely have protested. They'd say it couldn't be done, that the impossible was being expected of them, that conditions have to be just so in order for flowers to flourish, and that a concrete balcony was hopeless, hopeless, hopeless.

But there it was.

And here are these students in our classes, some from fertile soil who will take our teaching and yield goodness a hundred-fold. Others are surrounded by thorns, others are on rocky soil, but somewhere, somehow, they all have the potential for roots, for growth, and for harvest. We don't know how that can be, nor for whom, but we know it is possible, because as children of God we are constantly aware of miracles.

And we know this for certain: none of them will blossom without the seed. That's our job. Tend it well.

Suggested prayer: Sometimes, God, I am overwhelmed by all that I want to solve and cure for my students. Give me the grace and wisdom to do my part with faith and love, and trust their lives to You. Amen.

Daily reminder: *Sow the seed.*

Fear Not: Luke 2:8-20

"But the angel said to them, 'Do not be afraid; for see — I am bringing you good news of great joy for all the people.'" (Luke 2:10)

Imagine a quiet night in the fields suddenly ripped open by a messenger straight from God. This is no sweet Italian cherub: She is the power of eternity incarnate, armed with the glory of the Lord. Tremble, tremble, tremble.

Of course the shepherds were scared. Maybe they thought the angel had come to slay them, as had happened in the Passover story. Or maybe they feared they would be given a great burden or forced to wrestle all night, as had Moses and Jacob.

But they were given life, not death, and a simple task without a fight — go see a baby. "Good news of great joy." I doubt they were ever afraid again in their lives.

The angel's first words, "Do not be afraid," were repeated often by the child she announced. Over and over, in life and after his resurrection, Jesus tells his followers (that's us) to "Fear not." God has in Christ triumphed over all we could possibly fear, even over death. There is nothing left to be afraid of, not even angels.

Even though I know "perfect love casts out fear," I also know what panic feels like. For example: While living in Puerto Vallarta, Mexico, my children and I went with a church group to a concert in Guadalajara's massive bull ring. In the mob we became separated from our friends, and spent a miserable hour in the cold dark rain. Not only did I not know where our group was, I didn't know how to get back to the bus, either, and my Spanish was pathetic. I prayed, of course: "God, we are lost and alone and I am frightened. Help us find our way." The clear answer was, "Go get something to eat." It was so ridiculous that I ignored it for a while, but eventually I gave in. We wandered around until we found a man selling beautiful bread. At that very moment, a member of our group walked by and told us where everyone was. Great joy!

Here's the strange part: Not two minutes later, a strange woman came up to me and said, "Aren't you with the group from Puerto Vallarta? I'm so glad I found you! I've been wandering around lost!" I could tell she had been crying. And I confidently said, "There's nothing to be afraid of: let me show you where we belong." I heard an angel, I met an angel, I was an angel.

Then my children and I shared the bread, and it was the most delicious thing I've ever tasted. Then we went to the concert, and I've never sung "Alleluia" so loudly before or since.

That's how it works. A life of faith probably will hold moments of fear and anxiety, but it also holds the key to transcendence: When we obey the voice of God, we lead not only ourselves, but others, to a safe place where we belong. To friends, to communion, to a manger.

There are doubtless lost children in your classes who live in nearly constant fear of real or imagined terrors. What good news can you give them? What great joy do they see in you? Are you a person of courageous faith? If you are instead captive, stunted, or oppressed by your own fears, now is the time to bow down and listen, listen hard to the voice that says, "Do not be afraid." Then rise up and follow.

Suggested prayer: Mighty God, the world is full of danger and sorrow. Teach me to live without fear, confident in the good news that overcomes the world. Amen.

Daily reminder: *Do not be afraid.*

Authority And Demons: Luke 4:31-37

"They were astounded at his teaching, because he spoke with authority." (Luke 4:32)

I had a young colleague once who believed students should respect her simply because she was their teacher. Period. She was wrong.

Respect is not something that should be given to anyone simply because they are in a position of authority. A brief reflection will prove that plenty of people with earthly power don't deserve our respect. Blind obedience is not a Christian virtue, and deep respect needs to be earned.

To be sure, there is a level of respect "earned" simply by being a child of God, whether one be the teacher, the bus driver, or the kid next to us picking his nose. But the level of respect that means, "Here is someone I will believe, obey, and fully trust" is not to be given, or assumed, lightly.

Jesus inspired that kind of respect because he spoke with "authority." In other words, he spoke with a sureness of truth that only comes from being rooted in Eternal Being. His words were manifested in deeds of healing, nurturing, and inclusion.

By the same token, we speak with authority when we are sure of what we know, believe, and ask of our students and ourselves. Our words, too, are made manifest when we cast out demons.

If you think demons don't really exist, you clearly don't pay much attention to the world around you. Ignorance, oppression, fear, hatred, exploitation – surely these are very real demonic forces at work in our world. Does your teaching cast them out or invite them in? By these fruits will your authority be clear and respect earned.

A word of caution: Speaking with Godly authority invites earthly dangers from two mighty forces. Jesus may have been treated with awe by his followers, but he was feared and killed by others who felt their own authority threatened by this higher power. Something similar may happen to you. I have had more than one disagreement with administrators, for example, when I felt my students were being mistreated or in some way failed. I would like to say I have always been unfailingly polite and professional in these exchanges, but they may not agree!

The other danger comes from the demons themselves, who do not wish to be cast out. Ignorance, fear, and hatred will not fade quietly or willingly. But the Bible tells us that "with authority and power he [Jesus] commands the unclean spirits, and out they come!" (Luke 4:36). The same power is given to us as followers of Christ, if we but claim it. Do you for a moment believe God wants us to ignore, flee from, or bow down to the evil forces in the world – or even in our classrooms? No. We are to speak with the authority God has granted us through Christ, and if we are true and steadfast, acts of healing, nurturing, and inclusion will follow.

Will we then be respected by the world? By some people, yes. By others, no. But if we stand tall in the authority of God, it doesn't really matter.

Suggested prayer: When I feel encircled by the demons of this world, give me the strength, wisdom, and love to cast them out. Grant me the authority that only comes from respecting Your will. Amen.

Daily reminder: *Silence the demons.*

Level Ground: Luke 6:12-19

"He came down with them and stood on a level place, with a great crowd of his disciples..." (Luke 6:17)

Mountaintops play an important role in scripture as the meeting place of human and divine. Consider Mount Sinai, where Moses received the Ten Commandments. And Jesus often went "up to the mountain" to pray.

In modern parlance, a "mountaintop experience" means not a geographic reality, but a time of insight and inspiration, either spiritually or emotionally. Twelve years ago I was in a car accident while seven months pregnant, and the ecstasy I felt afterwards merely by being alive with a healthy baby inside me was certainly a "high."

I'm still alive, and my baby is now a brilliant seventh-grader, but that feeling of ecstasy was gone after the first 24 hours. We don't stay on the mountaintops, do we?

It may help to know that Jesus didn't stay there, either. What he gained on the mountain wasn't hoarded or lost there; instead, he brought that communion, wisdom, and peace with him down to level ground, and shared it with crowds through words and actions as "power came out from him." His night of prayer led to days of work.

The same challenge is set for us. I am fond of the phrase "green beans and dirty diapers," which I first read in a Buddhist context. It means that prayer and meditation are excellent, worthy, needful activities, but time must also be spent cooking meals and changing diapers. In other words, a balance must be struck between the divine and mundane, between the mountaintops we aspire to and the level ground we live on.

Achieving this balance is in large part a matter of discipline. I speak to myself now, because self-discipline is something I lack. As a working mother of three, I have to force myself to spend quiet time alone with God, but as a Christian I know it is the most important time of my day. If I want to be a loving, patient, wise and flowing fountain for my students, family, and colleagues, I must go to the mountain daily. There is no other source of power.

Too many Christians make the Sunday mistake: They believe that an hour in the pew every week will see them through. It's a good start, but it isn't nearly enough. You do well to also spend some time every week alone or in small groups with devotionals, such as this one, but that isn't enough, either. Daily Bible reading is excellent, but that isn't enough, either.

Going up to the mountain isn't a passive exercise. It's not about just reading something, or listening to someone else speaking. It's about yearning toward and obeying God at your own unique gut-soul level. Jesus spent all night there before he called his disciples, so when he called them, he was sure. There's a wisdom gained on the mountain that can't be found elsewhere, and it stays with you.

No human being can tell you how or where to reach God's heights, but through your own faith, patience, and discipline, the Holy Spirit will guide you. You'll know when you reach the summit, and others will know when you return to level ground.

Suggested prayer: This world is often rough going, God, and I want to transcend it all in Your embrace. Lead me to the mountaintop, and grant me the grace to share what I know there with the world. Amen.

Daily reminder: *Nights of prayer, days of work.*

The Resurrection Of The Living: Luke 8:40-42, 49-56

"But he [Jesus] took her by the hand and called out, 'Child, get up!' Her spirit returned, and she got up at once." (Luke 8:54-55)

The resurrection of the dead is something I look forward to some day. But the resurrection of the living seems more important at the moment.

We ought to live until the day we die, but many (most?) people choose to check out early. They breathe, walk, eat, earn money, and maybe even look good, but their spirits have left.

Maybe when a person decides that this world and its desires comprise all reality, their spirit is pushed out or swallowed by their materialism. Or maybe spirits shrivel down to a raisin after years of withering neglect. Or maybe spirits can make their own decisions, and they get fed up after awhile with the life they're being made to live, and leave. There could be all kinds of reasons for the living dead.

I know a little about this from personal experience. Depression runs in my family, but I was more or less fine until menopause hit. That's when I tried to kill my spirit but not my body. After a year of antidepressants and a leveling of hormones, I can look back at the experience, shudder, analyze it, and give thanks.

I tried to kill my spirit by giving up and giving in to mediocrity. In today's scripture reading, the young girl has taken to her bed and is assumed to be dying. I could have happily done the same thing, but I have children that kept me at least upright and moving. I now recall, as if from a movie, a woman who looks just like me burning all her manuscripts in a solemn ritual to deny her gifts. There's not much behind her eyes, and her beloved husband shrinks away from her. She's 46 years old, but feels ancient and hopeless.

You can't tell me that spirits don't leave.

Look carefully around your classroom if you don't believe me. When I have junior high students it really stands out: On the opposite end of the hormone rages, they too are tempted to give up and give in to whatever seems easiest at hand. Despair, angst, self-hatred, annihilation: it's all there. Some days, the pain in the room is nearly unbearable. It's a miracle any of us survive adolescence.

I am equally convinced, however, that spirits return. In my case, I am thankful to an insightful doctor, my own morbid wit, and a patient husband. But the resurrection point was at the command of the same voice that said, "Child, get up!" thousands of years ago. It's the same voice, the same message, the same result. "Her spirit returned."

Note that Jairus's daughter could not pray for her own recovery. Instead, her father, who clearly loved her, interceded on her behalf. "He fell at Jesus' feet and begged him to come to his house." And Jesus did.

We need to do the same thing for each other. Those of us who are well and strong – especially those of us who have made it through the dark night of the soul – need to fall on our knees on behalf of those whose spirits are threatened, damaged, or lost. Maybe we need to seek out a doctor, social worker, or counselor for them. But we also need to seek the one who commands spirits, to demand recovery, return, and resurrection to life.

Suggested prayer: I lift up today _____, whose spirit is weak, lost, or fleeing. Revive them, oh God! Command their spirit to rise up. Again and again, amen.

Daily reminder: *Child, get up!*

Treasure: Luke 12:22-34

"Make purses for yourselves that do not wear out, an unfailing treasure in heaven, where no thief comes near and no moth destroys." (*Luke 12: 33*)

My mother, who grew up in the Depression, was a great worrier. Even when she became solidly middle class, she kept a spare freezer full of bread and meat, just in case.

I grew up at a very different time, and have never been hungry for more than 15 minutes. I can dare to think of my mother as a needlessly fearful worry-wart. I'm certainly not like that.

Or am I? Today's scripture reading says, "Do not keep striving for what you are to eat and what you are to drink." Should it stop there? What else do we strive for? Love? Power? Security? Approval? There are other kinds of purses, other sorts of hoardings and fears and greed.

Jesus preached a culture of plenty, a kingdom of God where everything is given – *everything* – freely and plentifully. The ravens and the lilies have learned the secret of confidently accepting all gifts, and Jesus invites us to do the same.

Consider this small excerpt from the first verse: "Do not worry about your life." What do you need for your life? Whatever the answer, God offers it.

A short lesson in economics: Until the 18th century, wealth was considered limited. If you wanted to gain, someone else had to lose. In that scenario, acquiring a treasure meant taking it from others.

This train of thought came under attack in the 18th century when it was shown that wealth can be generated through initiative and participation in economies.

The analogy to the kingdom is clear. Some people fear that the treasures of God are limited: love, mercy, grace, forgiveness, wisdom, courage, justice. If others have these gifts, they must have taken them from us. If we have them, we must carefully guard and protect them.

But it isn't like that at all. The treasure of God is unlimited, and its manifestation only grows through our initiative and participation. In a culture of poverty, we hold fast to whatever we can gain. In a culture of plenty, we are free to live in outrageous generosity.

My mother didn't just hoard food. She was likewise careful with love, doling out only small bits at a time. I used to think of her as cold, but now I see that she simply shared the root disease of humanity: fear.

Your students and colleagues may have this mindset also. They worry about their popularity, their friends, their jobs, their grades, maybe even their food, drink, and clothing. They are worried that someone will take the good away from them. They are worried about starving, maybe not in body, but in spirit.

As children of the kingdom, we are called to live exemplary lives. We are here to testify that when we share the treasures of God, they are not spent. They grow, here and in heaven, unfailingly.

Suggested prayer: Generous God, there are times when I want to hoard all the goodness You have given me. Lead me to a generous heart and spirit, sharing Your bounty. Amen.

Daily reminder: *All these things will be given to you.*

Lost Sheep: Luke 15:1-10

"Rejoice with me, for I have found my sheep that was lost."
(Luke 15:6)

Frankly, I know a lot of people who would have stayed with the 99 sheep and let the lost one meet its own fate in the wilderness. I can even imagine their excuses:

"Who knows what the other 99 would have done while I was gone!"

"It's the stupid sheep's own fault for getting lost in the first place."

"I hear there are lions out there! And it was about to get dark. And I twisted my ankle last week. And ..."

"What lost sheep? I counted 100."

I know other people, and I'm one of them, who would rather prevent the whole lost thing from the outset, so we'd have well trained herd dogs to keep the sheep together. One dog would be in front as a guide, and others would be along the side or at the back of the flock to keep strays and stragglers where they belong. We would love our animals.

If a dog or sheep was lost, we'd look for it. If an animal was injured, we'd care for it, even if it meant carrying it in our arms through the desert. I hope I'm like that.

Then there are students. Out of any group of 100, we all know there's more than one lost soul. Maybe their body is sitting in front of us, but they might as well be wandering the wilderness. Their minds and souls are absent for so many reasons, from existential despair to raging hormones. And it's dark and scary out there.

How do we go after them?

There are, I believe two possible responses, relating back to the shepherd and her dogs. As individuals, it is so important that students know we care about them personally. My own elementary children adore their teachers, and will repeat every little compliment given to them. At the junior high and high school levels, I have individual conferences with each of my students every grading period (that's why God made movies for the other 99 to watch). Three minutes of private communication make a huge difference, especially when affirmations are given.

I think of a girl who really struggled in my history class. She was lousy at academics but wonderful at art. I invited her to present a research project as a cartoon, and it gave me an opportunity to praise her gifts. It didn't change her attitude toward book-learning, but at least for a time, she was found.

The herd dogs represent a group approach to seeking out the lost. I think of another student who several of us suspected was abusing drugs. No teacher wants to confront parents alone on such a topic, so we set up a group meeting with his parents and the school counselor. Each of us, without mentioning the "d" word, voiced our concerns about their son's behavior. By the end of the meeting, the mother said they had wondered about drug abuse. We had references ready to hand to her.

Teachers have a hundred excuses not to seek out the lost, and I've used a few myself. But we have only one Gospel, and it couldn't be clearer.

Suggested prayer: Dear God, I think of my student _____ who is sad and lost. Lead me to help him (her) find their way home to You and Your will for their life. Amen.
Daily Reminder: *Go after the one that is lost.*

Thank God: Luke 17:11-19

"He prostrated himself at Jesus' feet and thanked him."
(Luke 17:16)

As I approached today's scripture, I thought of this wonderful piece of advice attributed to Shawnee Chief Tecumseh: "When you arise in the morning, give thanks for the food and for the joy of living. If you see no reason for giving thanks, the fault lies only in yourself." How can something so obvious and true be so often ignored?

In our own family, we say grace before meals, and have long given thanks for the day at bedtime. But we now give thanks for the day as it begins, as well, and ask for help in being the sort of people that God wants us to be. That makes five times a day that we say, "Thank you" to God. Is it enough?

No, it isn't. Consider the story of the lepers. Theirs was a shameful disease, afflicting every aspect of their lives – physically, socially, spiritually. To be cured of such a curse was not only to be relieved of discomfort or danger, but to enter into an entirely new way of being in the world. A cured leper was made whole in every way.

A person who has undergone such a drastic change would surely be aware of it for every moment of their lives. "Thank you" might be said once, but it would be lived constantly. The one who was cured prostrated himself once at Jesus' feet, but his spirit surely bowed in awe and gratitude forever.

The same needs to be true of our own thankfulness. I say the right words with my own children, but words alone aren't enough. We need to live our thankfulness. What does that mean?

I am beginning to cultivate a prostrate mindfulness. This involves a constant awareness of the one and only thing I am always willing to submit to: My God. Paradoxically, my body tends to stand a little taller when my spirit is bowed. When I make mistakes (this happens often), I am thankful for the chance to learn. When I do something right, I am thankful for the chance to serve and grow. When a gift is granted, it is easy to be thankful. When a gift is withheld or withdrawn, I am thankful for the options in my life (they are always there).

Note that I'm just beginning to do this. It's easy when things go well, and less so when life doesn't unfold as I'd planned or hoped. But I know that a key to true spiritual fulfillment is to accept all of life as a gift, not just the bits and pieces we prefer.

The ramifications for a classroom are clear: Of course I'm going to be thankful for sweet little Polly who does her work well and pays close attention. Who wouldn't appreciate such a perfect student? But what about the little brat in the back who never shuts up? It takes a Godly mind to be thankful for him, too.

Practice being cured of this world. Take whatever words of gratitude you've used, and live them.

Suggested prayer: God, thank You for the opportunity I have been given to teach. May I live out my gratitude with love, joy, and faith. Amen.

Daily reminder: *Thank you, thank you.*

Overcoming The Darkness: John 1:1-18

"The light shines in the darkness, and the darkness did not overcome it." (John 1:5)

I write this in a time of war, when young men and women leave their homes to journey to foreign places not knowing whether they will kill or be killed.

I write this at a time of violence in our own homes, when women are daily killed by the very men who pledged to love them forever, when children are mercilessly betrayed by the people who gave them life.

I write this at a time of national cynicism, when every word uttered by our leaders is subject to doubt and ridicule.

I write this at a time of rampant materialism, when the emptiness we feel is stuffed with possessions and addictions in a futile quest for fulfillment.

I write this, in other words, at any point in human history.

The darkness takes many forms, and it has always been here. Sometimes it threatens to engulf us – Stalinist Russia, for example – but there always seems to be a way out, a point of hope followed through until life seems, if not perfect, at least bearable.

How does that happen? How is the unfathomable darkness overcome?

Those of us who teach history know its lessons in hope: small bands of radicals, underground writers and printers, courageous martyrs, astounding revelations constantly repeated until they became manifest.

It was so with the early Church, living dangerously in a time of war, violence, poverty, oppression, and decadence. This was no breeding ground for a philosophy of eternal love and life, yet that's what happened. The darkness was as great then as it is now, perhaps more so. But nonetheless, the light came. The light shone.

There were those who wanted Jesus to be some sort of political rabble rouser, but political victories, as we all know, are short lived before the corruptive cycle of power begins again. That isn't the way to everlasting victory.

The light that we are called to follow does not *correct* the darkness, it *overcomes* it. What is the difference? It is, simply and profoundly, the cross.

Jesus didn't persuade Pontius Pilate to see the error of his ways, or calm the vicious crowd, or assuage the fear of his enemies. There were no debates or compromises. He was put to death, in an hour of despair the likes of which we may never know.

But the evil of this world was not and will not be triumphant, simply because the powers of this world are so limited. Have no doubt, the darkness is there, and we live and suffer through it. God forgive us, we even contribute to it at times. But God in Christ has overcome the world.

When we define our life by the darkness we meet, we are already defeated in mind and spirit. When instead we shape our life by the eternal light of grace and truth, then we know ourselves to be children of God. And we will not be overcome.

Suggested prayer: The world is heavy, God, and it weighs me down at times. Lead me to the truth of life, Your eternal light, that I may live in confident joy. Amen.

Daily reminder: *He gave [us] power to become children of God.*

A Well Within: John 4:7-30

"The water that I will give will become in them a spring of water gushing up to eternal life." (John 4:14)

My husband, a farmer, shakes his head every spring when I come home from the nursery laden with young flowers. He knows what will happen: I'll plant them, I'll water them for a week or two, and I'll forget about them. There are many dead flowers in our yard.

How many of our students are like that? Most of them were loved as babies. In early elementary they enthusiastically learned to read and add 2 + 2. Then too many of them go dry. Their spirits shrivel, their roots contract, their fruit dies before it flowers. How does that happen?

We don't always make the best choices for them, do we? For example, the difficult years of junior high are laden with spiritual, emotional, and physical minefields, and that's when they enter larger schools with more complex schedules and escalated academic demands. Their parents assume they are old enough to take care of themselves, for hours, for days and nights. The culture bombards them with cheap sexuality and materialism. We all forget to water them.

"Everyone who drinks of this water will be thirsty again," Jesus warned. And when our children thirst for love and meaning, they slake their need with what is offered: drugs, alcohol, promiscuity, apathy, self-destruction, exploitative accumulation of possessions and status. All those solutions work, momentarily. Then the children thirst, again.

So what do we do about it?

I believe radical structural changes are needed in education, but that's another book. We need to give a drink to the students we have right here, right now. There are three steps to doing this:

We cannot give what we do not have. If you have come this far in this book, it means you are committed to seeking a deep expression of your faith. Care for the well within you, that eternal spring. Visualize it in the morning and in your classes. You are a tree planted by the river of life. How amazing is that!

Lead students to discover, however you can, that the choices they make now influence what they will become later in life. I could take one of my dead flowers into class and say, "Okay, what did I do wrong?" After they all happily tell me, I'll assign an essay, "How is your life like a flower? What do you need to grow into the person you want to be?" This may sound elementary, but most adolescents don't make conscious choices or think through consequences. Simply inviting them to do so may make a difference.

Thirdly, pay attention to their answers. What do they really need? Find a way to give it to them. I teach literature, which is nothing less than teaching life, so I have many opportunities to invite students to explore their own spirits and futures. I cannot hand them a Bible in a public school, but I can offer them a cup of clear water. And that's the beginning of salvation.

Suggested prayer: I lift up my student _____, who I know is thirsting for meaning and love. May I be a servant of Your will for their life, a bearer of the cup. Amen.

Daily reminder: *A spring of water gushing up to eternal life.*

Hard To Believe: John 11:1-7; 17-45

"I am the resurrection and the life. Those who believe in me, even though they die, will live." (John 11:25)

Westerners raised with faith in science have a hard time accepting that not all causes and effects are known and predictable, so they find miracles hard to believe. "There's an explanation," they'll say.

I have heard this beautiful story about Lazarus "explained" by saying of course he wasn't really dead, or he was in cahoots with Jesus to fool people. That God incarnate was able to raise the dead is just unbelievable to many people.

But when the miracle is personal, it's a different story. I have a friend who was diagnosed with an aggressive cancer in an advanced stage. "Miracle" is the word her doctor used when she was clean a year later.

I have another friend who was dying from a genetic kidney ailment until I heard a voice telling me to get tested. To make a long story short, she was my maid of honor five weeks after our transplant. She considered our match and her recovery a miracle.

You may have your own examples, from friends, family, or students. You've probably heard at least one of these:

"It's a miracle anyone survived the crash."

"I was told I couldn't have children, so she's my miracle baby."

"If that kid ever graduates, it'll be a miracle."

Such good things really do have a simple explanation: We live in a world of miracles.

To realize we don't know everything, let alone control life's events, is a liberating bit of knowledge. My favorite Shakespeare line is from *Hamlet*: "There are more things in heaven and earth, Horatio, than are dreamt of in your philosophy." I think of it every time I read an article by a scientist who is sure we're on the verge of knowing everything about anything. And I laugh.

I believe that humans are gifted with great intelligence, insight, and creativity. I also believe there are mysteries beyond our comprehension or even imagination. Such humility stands me well when, for example, I find myself analyzing my students or predicting their future.

Who am I to say they won't be resurrected in body, mind, or spirit?

Water into wine, banquets from a child's lunch, the sighted blind, demons exorcised, the dead raised. Why not? It's God we're talking about, not you and me or anything we can pin under a microscope, measure out, or in any way manipulate.

These are the miracles of God: Celebration, nurturance, healing, freedom, life. They all spring from love and they can't be explained but they aren't so hard to believe because you know you've experienced them yourself.

Lazarus was really dead. Jesus really raised him. The same thing will happen to you. Believe it.

Suggested prayer: Help my unbelief in life's profound wonder. Amen.
Daily reminder: *Life is a miracle.*

Love One Another: John 15:9-17

"This is my commandment, that you love one another as I have loved you." (John 15:12)

Christianity boils down to this, doesn't it? If we love one another as God loves us, we have everything else right.

The first step is to understand how God loves us. Jesus' life was a manifestation of God's universal, unconditional love. He didn't include the dispossessed, oppressed, and sinful as a grudging afterthought, but at the center of his banquet. He didn't love us as long as it was convenient or pleasant for him, but from the cross.

The second step is to understand who "one another" is for us. It is usually easy to love our friends and family. But faith challenges us to love everyone, and that's so much easier said than done.

Visualize the most difficult student you have ever had: Was he lazy, rude, violent, vulgar? Now imagine God loving him from the cross.

Why?

Maybe we can grasp that God loves everyone, but why is that true? I believe it goes back to the moment of creation, not of the world but of each human being in it. I believe that each of our souls contains a spark of the divine, a seed that can be nourished, rejected, or starved, but not fully destroyed. And that innate connection unites each of us to God, whether we realize it or not.

Many people reject God's love out of ignorance or choice, but believers are called to not only embrace it, but practice it.

It isn't enough to accept God's love for ourselves. We need to bear fruit of it as well.

Loving people certainly does not mean loving everything they do. The adage "Hate the sin, love the sinner" has a core value and truth. The difficult student can have thoughts and actions that are abhorrent to you, but God was still willing to die for him. The least you can do is share that love.

On the first day of every year, I tell all my students that I promise to love and respect them unless they give me a good reason not to, and so far, the reasons have been few and far between. When they do occur, I have had difficult relationships turn around with prayer. I do not ask that they suddenly change, but that God's love for them would be made manifest in my own life. It usually works.

An important note: Sometimes we need to love people from a distance. If a student is threatening or otherwise toxic to you or your class, Christ does not demand that we continue to allow them to be so. The love you bear yourself and others entails protection from physical, emotional, and spiritual harm. Godly love is a mighty force, not weak acquiescence.

The most difficult student I can think of physically assaulted me. He was promptly removed from my class, but I continued to pray for him. And my faith that God loves him is not shaken.

Suggested prayer: I give You thanks, God, for loving me throughout my life. Open my heart so that Your generous love will flow through me to others. In Christ's name, Amen.
Daily Reminder: *Love one another.*

Slaves And Children: Romans 8: 9-17

"For you did not receive a spirit of slavery to fall back into fear, but you have received a spirit of adoption. When we cry, 'Abba! Father!' it is that very Spirit bearing witness with our spirit that we are children of God." (Romans 8: 15-16)

Thanks be to God, the United States no longer suffers the enslavement of human beings, at least in the most literal, physical sense. But all too many of us chose to be captive to a wide range of masters, none of which deserve to hold the souls of the Godly.

Enslavement is obvious in addictions; other masters are subtler, and some, like the love of money, are actually praised in our culture. But if you live for anything outside yourself, you are a slave to it. Period. We cannot serve both God and _____ (fill in the blank).

Paul wrote of the great difference between a slave to fear and a child of God. In the former we live outwardly, striving constantly toward what we think we need: "I *must*," the captive says, "have that drink, that high, that promotion, that glory, ..." Such a spirit is held hostage to something that must be repeatedly attained to give life purpose and pleasure.

A child of God, on the other hand, already has everything she needs. Our purpose and pleasure are programmed into us, just as our earthly parents gave us green eyes or mahogany skin. It is not at all a matter of spirit as distinct from body, a split duality at war, but rather of spirit informing our physical existence, not the other way around.

Theologian Pierre Teilhard de Chardin wrote, "We are not human beings having a spiritual experience; we are spiritual beings having a human experience." Our spirits are eternally free in God, and that fact alone should give this human life joy and peace.

I write what I need to know, because sometimes I have a wicked temper and am all too familiar with the sloughs of despond. But not long ago my unconscious – my soul? – reminded me of this truth at my core.

To make a long story short, I drove an elderly couple to their home when they had been stranded on the highway. We were all basically monolingual – they in Spanish and I in English, so we didn't talk much. When I dropped them off, the gentleman tried to pay me, and I refused, saying, effortlessly, *"Yo vivo para Dios."* He looked surprised, whether at my faith or sudden sense in Spanish I do not know, but then this stranger gave me a hug, as did his wife. I sang all the way back to my home.

That is how I need to live, always: When the world offers temptation, refuse with a smile and affirm, "I live for God." So simple it's profound.

And in our classrooms: How tempting it is to make students think they should live for that A, that standardized test, that first place trophy, that 4.0, that class election, the star part in the play or on the field. Sure, they should do their best, not in order to be loved but because they are loved and supported and limitless. Do we clearly, humbly, love ourselves and others because we are all children of the same infinite, loving, powerful God? Do we invite others to the freedom of their amazing potential? Heirs with Christ – think of it.

Your glory, sisters and brothers, needs to show!

Suggested prayer: Abba! Father! My spirit lives in You – always has, always will. Amen.
Daily reminder: *Yo vivo para Dios.*

One Body: 1 Corinthians 12:4-31

"Now there are varieties of gifts, but the same Spirit; and there are varieties of services, but the same Lord; and there are varieties of activities, but it is the same God who activates all of them in everyone."
(1 Corinthians 12: 4-6)

My students love cooperative learning, but for years I was frustrated by how little work seemed to actually get done (despite lots of talking!). Then I finally hit on the members of the body idea, otherwise known as assigning tasks. If each person is given a specific role to fulfill, and those roles are properly taught and loudly appreciated, then the practical benefits of grouping increase a hundredfold.

Besides improved academic outcomes, cooperative learning also increases both self-confidence in students otherwise too shy to participate and humility in people like me who tend to take over. Changing tasks with each assignment also invites students to discover skills in themselves and others that had hitherto been dormant. For all these reasons, I now incorporate as much group work as I can in class.

What is true of best practices in teaching holds for the rest of life as well. Most goals are more easily and completely met when the processes to reach them are broken down and divided among workers. Such work is also more enjoyable when the workers support and applaud each other, no matter how small the task given.

The challenge both in and out of class is to keep from making a hierarchy of contributions, implying that one member is more important, and by implication more able, than another.

Rotating responsibilities should keep anyone from feeling like king or pawn.

A very special elementary student inadvertently taught me a direct lesson about working in groups. Lori is beautiful, loving, and autistic. She struggles in some academic areas, but the child is a gifted and enthusiastic actor. No matter what role she is given in plays, movies, or readers' theater, she is ecstatically delighted and gives it her very best. She is also generous with praise for others. I respect her greatly as a role model.

This is what Paul meant when he wrote to the church in Corinth that we are all members of the body of Christ. There was no ranking of gifts, but "to each is given the manifestation of the Spirit for the common good." Likewise, there was to be no "better than thou" attitude among Jews or Greeks, slaves or free, rich or poor, male or female, opposites in the cultural milieu but common members in faith. In this way, Christianity is like modern public education, inviting everyone to a leveled playing field.

Now quite obviously, some students are better at some things than at others, and some students excel far beyond their peers in some areas. But everyone can teach and learn, give and take, and work toward a common goal and their own personal bests. Leading students to know and share their gifts, to rely on and appreciate the gifts of others, to be part of something greater than themselves is not just good teaching: It's the Spirit at work in you.

Suggested prayer: Spirit of God, open my eyes and heart so that I will lead my students to recognize, develop, give, and receive the gifts You have given each of them. In gratitude, Amen.
Daily reminder: *Though many, we are one.*

What Are You Thinking? Philippians 4:4-9

"Finally, beloved, whatever is true, whatever is honorable, whatever is just, whatever is pure, whatever is pleasing, whatever is commendable, if there is any excellence and there is anything worthy of praise, think about these things." (Philippians 4:8)

Sometimes I get ideas stuck in my head about how lousy this or that is, or, more often, what a pathetic loser I am. I should've done that, I shouldn't have said that, I should have gone there, I shouldn't have eaten that ice cream ... The list seems endless, especially at 2 a.m. when all I really, really should do is sleep.

When negativity is on a continuous loop in your head, it's time to put in a new tape. I have been heard to say, "Attitude change, now!" to countless teens in my time. Astonishingly, it usually works. Most people, even 16-year-olds, agree once it's pointed out to them that they've let their inner critic, fretful imagination, or sour disposition go too far too long, again. They laugh at themselves and yes, change (for a while, anyway).

Christianity is nothing less than radical transformation of the inner self into a new creation, born of and living in God – a seismic attitude change. Even if no one else is awake to tell you to snap out of your gloom, doom, and self-damnation, the Lord is near. God did not put us here to be miserable and full of self-hate. We were put here to joyfully manifest the divine.

Like all worthy accomplishments, joy takes practice. For a week, notice when your mind starts down that dark and winding path that ends with something like, "I'm no good!" Then pull out Philippians 4:4-9 and do what it says. Rejoice always.

Keeping a journal could help. At the end of each day, write down at least three things you are thankful for. It could be quite ordinary, such as, "I had a delicious veggie sandwich for lunch." Or it could be extraordinary, like, "Everyone had their speech prepared in third period today." You will quickly realize that you missed a great many good moments back when you instead focused on the less than perfect aspects of your life and those around you.

Also, practice sincere affirmations of others. I have a colleague who is an expert at this. After a school program, for example, she will e-mail the teachers involved and tell them how much she enjoyed it, and she makes certain to cc everyone else. We are all uplifted by her kind acknowledgements, whether directed to us or not. Likewise, I make it a point to send positive messages home to parents on a regular basis. One surprised father told me he isn't reluctant to answer a call from school anymore – it might be *good* news about his (energetic) son!

Another idea is to keep a "happy box" of cards and notes from students, perfect teaching cartoons, acknowledgements from parents and supervisors, meaningful photos, etc. On those days when I feel like a failure, it helps to have solid evidence that actually, I'm good at this.

It is also sometimes necessary to seek professional help if the doldrums last for weeks on end. I was once told that a truly good Christian could pray her way out of clinical depression; maybe some can, but I've needed antidepressants at times. There's no shame to it.

However you get there, know that the goal for your life in God is joy and peace, for you, for those whose lives you touch, and for the world. What a thought. Amen.

Suggested prayer: Make me mindful, gracious God, of all the beauty and goodness that is mine for the notice. Thank You, Amen.

Daily reminder: *Rejoice in the Lord always.*

Meditations for Special Circumstances

Christmas: Matthew 1:18-25

"'... and they shall name him Emmanuel,' which means, 'God is with us.'" (Matthew 1:23)

Many years ago, when I was the parish minister, I was asked to direct the local elementary school's Christmas program, since I led the children's choir at church. The teacher who called added to the request, "Now, you know we can't have any religious music in the program." Not knowing any better, I agreed.

That was then. Last Christmas, in the same school, I led my own classes in singing Christmas songs from around the world, and Jesus was in several of them in several languages. Of course you can.

According to the Freedom Forum, "School concerts that present a variety of selections may include religious music. Concerts should avoid programs dominated by religious music, especially when these coincide with a particular religious holiday" ("A Teacher's Guide to Religion in the Public Schools," www.freedomforum.org). In other words, though Christian music cannot form the largest part of a school concert, it needn't be omitted altogether; teaching the history and traditions of widely celebrated holidays (holy-days) should not disregard details such as, for example, why it's called Christ-mas. As the U.S. Department of Education points out, though we cannot *preach* religion in schools run by a pluralistic democracy, we can (and should) *teach* it. Ignorance is not a civic virtue.

Unfortunately, too many teachers (and boards of education) think schools should be religion-free zones to the point that any expression of faith is not tolerated (unless it's exotic). The end result for December has been, in my suffered experience, sticky sweet Santa shows that celebrate (dare I say preach?) the acquisition of goodies. You have the right to politely refuse to participate in such a charade, saying something like, "I must decline participation in the program 'Christmas Means Candy!' on the grounds that it mocks the true meaning of the holiday according to my personal beliefs."

Speaking of materialism, what about classroom parties? Because some of my students come from impoverished families, I don't agree to gift exchanges between students, but I do give each of my students a small gift on the last day before break (this year it was a book of poetry), and we have cookies and punch; Charles Dickens' "A Christmas Carol" fits in the week somewhere – I do prefer Christmas ghosts to Santa!

Some schools have solved the issue of keeping everyone happy about Christmas by ignoring it altogether, calling the last half of December "winter break" and holding no observance. I actually prefer this to pushing a materialistic secular agenda, and it is a worthy suggestion for a Christian to make in a school that will not allow any religious expression.

That certainly doesn't mean you don't celebrate Christmas outside your own home – be involved with your church, and make sure that any Christmas observance there is held with arms wide open to the community. Spread the Good News - God is with us indeed!

Conflicts With Colleagues:
Matthew 18:15-18; Luke 17:3-4

"If another member of the church sins against you, go and point out the fault when the two of you are alone." (Matthew 18:15)

How is a Christian to respond when inevitable conflicts arise with colleagues in the workplace? "Turning the other cheek" walks a fine line between being a loving, forgiving person and a patsy. Nothing in the Gospels requires us to be victimized by the world.

I cannot stand being lied to or about, and like many people, my brain freezes when I'm angry – I just can't think of the right thing to say or do. Fortunately, the Bible outlines the process for us. We could summarize the Matthew excerpt thus, substituting school for church:

If someone offends you, go to them in private and calmly state your concern, speaking the truth in love (ask God to love them through you if you can't do it alone). If you are too upset to trust yourself, there is nothing wrong with writing a letter and then reading it aloud to them. That sort of paper trail also makes misunderstandings less likely.

If they refuse to listen to you, or flagrantly lie to your face, then return another day with a witness. The witness does not need to say anything. This also works, incidentally, in conflicts with parents. I have had principals and counselors sit as silent witnesses to tense conferences, and it helps enormously, both in monitoring the situation and in providing a reality check afterwards. The witness needs to be someone whose confidentiality you trust; this can't be fodder for the teacher's lounge.

If the offender still does not realize how they have wronged you, or feels you deserve your pain, it is time to take the matter to the next step in your school's administrative hierarchy and file a formal complaint. Have ready a written summary of the steps you have taken thus far.

Your school should have a grievance policy for more serious situations, but for one-to-one issues, Jesus' process works as well now as it did 2,000 years ago, of course.

I rarely get seriously upset with colleagues for long, but when I do, I get on my knees, and "love them" is the answer I'm always stuck with. I have to admit, it works. This brings us to Luke 17:3: "If there is repentance, you must forgive." We need to determine for ourselves whether repentance is genuine, and if it is, then forgiveness must follow.

The form of forgiveness must never condone the sin; it needs to acknowledge the error and accept the intention that it won't happen again. If someone is sorry they hurt you, for heaven's sake don't say, "That's okay." It wasn't okay. Say instead, "I'm glad you realize that was hurtful, and I forgive you and trust it won't happen again."

(An annoying voice is telling me I can't be a hypocrite: I once refused to meet with a young man who physically attacked me and later said he wanted to apologize, but I know that forgiveness in such situations is often grossly misinterpreted by the offender. There's nothing wrong in such cases with using an intermediary.)

One of the great things about teaching is a nice long break before each brand new year. Doesn't September feel like a clean slate? If you've had conflicts with colleagues in the past, give any remaining rancor and pain to God, and begin again. Jesus says that when conflicts are settled, you have "regained that one." As importantly, when you follow God's word, you regain your own peace.

Death Of A Student Or Colleague: John 20:11-19

"Peace be with you." *(John 20:19)*

If you turned to this page because tragedy just struck, my heart goes out to you. The death of someone in a school community shakes the foundations, especially if it is a child. What do you do? What do you say?

Our natural reactions with family, personal friends, and fellow Christians will need to be checked in a school setting. Prayer is an instant reaction for believers in times of crisis, but care should be taken to guarantee it couldn't possibly be misconstrued in a public setting.

Once we were rehearsing a play when word came that the star's brother had just been in a serious car accident. I knew the family to be devout Catholics, and I quietly asked my student if she would like to pray before she left for the hospital. She nodded yes through her tears, and I called over two other students, friends of hers who I knew to be Christian. The four of us went into another room, and we surrounded her in brief but heartfelt prayer.

A colleague who heard of this said teachers should *never* pray with students, but I believe the guidelines I followed were sufficient to rule out any possible sense of coercion. It was a moment of crisis, I knew all the students involved, I privately asked the person in need if they would like to pray, and the actual praying took place privately, away from the sight or hearing of anyone else. Of course, private, silent prayer is always acceptable to God and whoever thinks they're in charge of you.

When comforting those who do not have faith, less is more. Holding hands, a hug for those you know well, and simply listening and empathizing will speak volumes. If you want to share the promise of the resurrection with specific individuals, it needs to be away from school, and how much you say needs to be guided by how much they clearly want to hear. If students in class ask your opinion on life and death issues, concise answers to the point will suffice, and if they want to dig deeper, invite them to speak to you outside of class.

I know this flies in the face of evangelical ardor, but there are sound reasons why employees of public schools cannot preach to a captive audience (and "preaching" can be widely interpreted). Imagine that a teacher had beliefs very different from your own, and your child was forced to listen to them daily. As a parent, you want to nurture your own child's faith, and as Americans we all need to respect the choices other individuals make, even when we believe them to be misguided.

If at all possible, attend the funeral, no matter what church, synagogue, temple, mosque, or public hall it is held in; your respectful presence is a witness. It's always appropriate to send a note to the family and closest friends of the deceased sharing a fond memory you have. A card with a Bible verse or religious image on it would be acceptable when sent from your home address, not the school's.

Having said all that, I once preached in school, while officiating the funeral of my beloved and very popular 16-year-old neighbor. Because of the expected crowd, the funeral was held in the school gym instead of our small church. I made it clear to the principal that it would be a religious service. About 800 people attended, including many students from surrounding schools. I witnessed to my young friend's faith and my conviction that he was in the arms of God. A friend later told me she had walked in torn by grief and walked out feeling loved.

That's the peace of God. However you can, share it.

Evaluations: Matthew 5:1-16

"Blessed are you..." (Matthew 5:11)

I'm a perfectionist who doesn't take criticism well, especially when it isn't valid. Because I take great pride in my teaching, the evaluation process has been emotional at times. But after years of being evaluated, I've learned the secrets to equanimity even in the face of the most ill-informed principal.

First, practice the presence of Christ. Imagine that at any moment Jesus himself, the ultimate teacher, might walk into your classroom, sit down, and evaluate your performance after observing you teach and interact with your students for an hour ("Yikes!" I would say some days). Be ready for it always with thoughtful, supported lesson plans, a positive attitude, and genuine love for students and learning. If you can handle the divine on a moment's notice, you can handle any mere mortal who makes an appointment.

Speaking of mere mortals, have mercy on the evaluator. Few have mastered the art of critiquing the worth of people they've actually seen at work a few hours a year at most. Not only is limited time at fault, but principals come to those observations with the baggage of their own experience intact. Early in my career, my principal was very negative about the noise level in my room: "Your students talk too much!" he complained. They had been working in cooperative groups on a novel we were reading, and I thought the lesson went splendidly. But he thought students should sit forward in rows silently listening to the teacher lecture; my class looked plain chaotic to him. I didn't have the confidence back then to argue with him, which brings me to my last point.

Be prepared to explain yourself, professionally and calmly. Every contract I've had allows teachers to attach written responses to evaluations. Don't be shy about defending your decisions and actions, backing them up with research or policy where possible; being "meek" doesn't mean allowing other people to run over you. If an evaluation is really out of line, consider going to the next step in the hierarchy, again with prepared written support of your work. If you know you're tending the vineyards faithfully, you have nothing to fear.

On the other hand, I have also learned to graciously accept creative criticism that will help my teaching. "That's a wonderful idea, thank you," is all that need be said in response to a good suggestion from a supervisor or colleague. Then follow up that conversation with a quick e-mail on outcome: "I tried your idea today and the results were very positive. Thank you again for ..." *That's* meekness with a blessing.

Finally, do not approach observations and evaluations with dread. Christ is indeed always in your room, but your principal is not God incarnate. No matter what anyone else thinks, you are blessed because of who and whose you are: a child of God, the salt and light of the world. Remember the woman who stood tall when she felt the power of God in Christ? We are all meant to do the same.

Work for God's pleasure, and blessings will follow.

Lay-Offs: Jeremiah 29:10-14

While I was writing this book, I faced losing my job due to budget cuts; I am happy to say that my contract was continued, but only after my soul found peace. The following essay was published in the June-July 2009 issue of The United Church of Christ News. *I repeat it here to help anyone who may be in the same situation.*

As I write this in May 2009, I face losing my teaching job due to a budget crisis. After years with the same school district, last year I left a job I loved in order to move to the same school my own children attend, with my young daughter in my class. I was getting the hang of the new place when I learned that, as the last teacher hired, I would be the first to go.

Every school in our area is in the same situation, so there are no openings. The range of emotions I have experienced go from bad to worse. There have been crying fits that come on suddenly and last too long. I feel betrayed, unwanted, and so, so stupid for ever leaving a secure harbor. I feel painfully invisible when résumés I send are not even acknowledged.

I have two master's degrees, am National Board certified, hold multiple endorsements, and have ten years of exceptional teaching experience. And it looks like I'm going on unemployment.

I have been bleeding, kicking, and screaming inside because my identity was being taken from me. I am called to teach more strongly than I was to parish ministry many years ago, and who am I without that?

This is where God comes in.

Yesterday was hellish, and today both of my sons were confirmed in church. The confirmands each presented a verse that summarized their faith, and my eldest chose Jeremiah 29:11: "For surely I know the plans I have for you, says the Lord, plans for your welfare and not for harm, to give you a future with hope."

Then at one point our minister said something about the young people being "called to be disciples of Christ."

Though intended for teenagers, both pronouncements spoke deeply to the middle-aged woman in the third row facing an uncertain future.

With shame, I remember my supportive husband trying to console me just yesterday with what I rudely dismissed as a worn cliché: "Maybe God is leading you to another calling."

With even more embarrassment, I remember standing at a guest pulpit not long ago preaching from my favorite epistle: "Beloved, we are God's children now; what we will be has not yet been revealed" (1 John 3:2).

In repentance, I confess to falling into the decidedly American trap of confusing *self* with a job title and paycheck. Faith demands instead an embrace of my soul as the eternal God's disciple and daughter with a future of hope that will be revealed in its own time. I've been toying with publishing for years; could I not turn this grave disappointment into opportunity for growth?

I wish I could say I am now suddenly full of peace and clarity, but I'm too much of a control freak for that. I still grieve losing my students and income.

But I no longer mourn the negation of my spirit, and I do realize, finally, that I certainly never left my safe harbor; indeed, I am moored for all life to come.

And to anyone else in this painful situation, I give my blessing, empathy, and invitation to rediscover your center within the Truth this world can never take away.

Sports: 1 Corinthians 6:19-20, 9:24-27

"For you were bought with a price; therefore glorify God in your body."
(1 Corinthians 6:20)

Chess is my idea of a good sport, but I live with athletes and have thus modified my thinking about sports programs in school. I used to think of football, volleyball, track, basketball, etc. as bothersome distractions from the real business of learning, and I thought of coaches (forgive me) as a slight step above Neanderthals – before my [brilliant] beloved became one. Now I see the good, even Godly, side of athletics.

Paul used athletic metaphors to explain the self-control and perseverance needed for a Christian life, and exalted the physical body as the temple of the Holy Spirit. As a citizen of ancient Rome, he would have taken for granted the desire for "a healthy mind in a healthy body." He might have added a healthy soul, too.

As a coach, you have an obligation to instill in your students the self-discipline required to achieve their personal best, and to relate that to the rest of their lives; this can easily be done without direct reference to religion. I know that many young people trust their coaches as advisors; pray that you may help lead them on their best life path.

You could go a step further in inspiring the faith of young people through athletics if you could sponsor a club such as Fellowship of Christian Athletes; be very careful, though, not to show undue partiality to fellow believers when making team decisions.

As a Christian you also need to put the brakes on out-of-control competition that glorifies violence and hatred of the enemy; we have too much of that in our culture already. Athletes should respect their opponents' skills and play for the shared love of the game, not the desired annihilation of the other. I've been in schools that line their halls with hateful propaganda every homecoming; what is that teaching? I've heard coaches think it's good for kids to be yelled at and belittled, even cursed in the heat of the moment. No, it isn't. Be the change that needs to happen around these issues.

If you are not a coach, there are good reasons for supporting without elevating athletes in your classes. Students with bodily-kinesthetic intelligence should be allowed to use that in writing and research assignments. Throw out the "dumb jock" stereotype, but don't give in to the opposite extreme of hero worship.

And whether you are a coach or not, your own body teaches students more than you want to admit. I'm once again writing to myself, because I need to exercise more, eat less, blah, blah, blah. I *need* to because (1) my body is the temple of the Holy Spirit and (2) my students learn from everything I say and do (and don't do). I teach elementary these days, including, God help me, physical education, and I'm making a vow right now to get out on the playing field with my students next year.

You can't expect students to do or be something you aren't willing to do or be yourself. So get out there and "run with perseverance the race that is set before us, looking to Jesus the pioneer and perfecter of our faith" (Hebrews 12:1b-2).

Amen.